W9-ARB-202

A Migrant with Hope

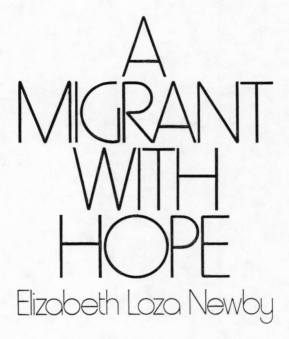

A MIGRANT WITH HOPE

Elizabeth Loza Newby

LIBRARY
BRYAN COLLEGE
DAYTON, TN. 37321

Broadman Press
Nashville, Tennessee

58889

© Copyright 1977 ● Broadman Press.

All rights reserved.

4272-18

ISBN: 0-8054-7218-5

Dewey Decimal Classification: B

Subject Headings: NEWBY, ELIZABETH//MIGRANT LABOR—BIOGRAPHY

Library of Congress Catalog Card Number: 76-053980

Printed in the United States of America

This book is dedicated to
my daughter, Alicia Marie,
who will never live the
life of a migrant girl

All Scripture verses are taken from the Revised Standard Version of the Bible.

Foreword

Elizabeth Newby is a great person. Starting with the severest handicap, both socially and educationally, she has achieved a level of excellence in her total life. She is a good wife, a good mother, a good thinker, and, finally, a good writer. In personal contacts she wins all hearts by the genuineness of her affection.

Why has Elizabeth moved so far so fast, in spite of an incredibly poor start? Part of the reason lies in her complete lack of self-pity and her refusal to let her environment become an excuse for failure. She believes that people can change, and she has provided a demonstration of her conviction. She shows that it is not necessary to be culture bound. Her entire experience is a challenge to the popular doctrine of cultural determinism, which is often employed in our generation to deny responsibility. Of course, says Elizabeth, she began with both economic and cultural poverty. But does she stop there? Emphatically, she does not! She knows that conversion is a fact and that it can take many forms, one of which is her own.

The migrant workers constitute a subculture which, up to now, has produced almost no literature of its own. The migrants have, of course, been written about; but heretofore they have not, for the most part, written about themselves. Elizabeth is in the strategic position of one who has escaped the usual consequences of cultural deprivation sufficiently to be able to write about it, but has remained close enough to her origins to be able to speak understandingly and with remarkable compassion and gratitude. Her references to a few obscure but effective teachers are deeply moving, and her portraits of her parents are not easily forgotten.

I have counted it a privilege to be Mrs. Newby's teacher, partly because I look upon this as only the first of many books from her pen. The probability that authorship is her vocation is very great. In helping her I have had a sense of being a participant in the ministry of multiplication. My own assistance has come about because of my responsibility in the recently organized Yokefellow Academy. This is a new kind of educational venture devoted to the discovery, nurture, and guidance of spiritual potential regardless of sex, age, location, or scholastic standing. Mrs. Newby's book is the first publication to appear as a result of the formation of the Academy.

It would be a mistake to suppose that Mrs. Newby's book is just one more in the array of books that represent the cult of personal exposure. Hers is different in kind! Her message is one of hope to all who feel caught in the net of determinism. The author is seeking to say to all who will read, and especially to all who, like herself, are still young, that it is possible to turn disabilities into opportunities. She hopes, by telling her story, not primarily to entertain or to shock, but to encourage thousands of persons who are now discouraged. The story belongs in one sense to the literature of witness; but in a far deeper sense, it belongs to the literature of hope.

D. ELTON TRUEBLOOD

Preface

My life as a young girl was far from representative of American experience, for I belonged to a minority of a minority. Our experience is one that deserves to be more widely known and understood. I believe I can help readers to understand it because for thirteen years I lived in the back of a 1942 Army surplus truck, which served us as a home, while we followed the annual harvest of cotton, sugar beets, strawberries, cantaloupe, lettuce, and grapes back and forth across America. All of the experiences described in the following pages are factual; I lived them! However, because of my desire to protect the anonymity of my parents, I have avoided mentioning the names of particular towns and localities.

My purpose in writing this book is to acquaint the reader with the real-life struggles and adventures of a girl growing up in a migrant farm worker's family. It is not a book dealing with farm worker unionization or the Chicano movement. Abundant material on these subjects has already been produced and is readily available to anyone wishing to learn more about them. All that I am trying to do in this book is to tell, in a truly simple way, about many of the experiences that come with the life of a migrant and about how one girl, Elizabeth, was finally able to escape from a life that was severely restricted.

The first chapter deals with my entry into the migrant community and my experiences while a part of the roving caravan. In the second chapter I try to describe how my family became settled migrants, reporting the experiences that came with our new life in a home on solid ground. The third chapter tells about my struggles for independence, including my disownment by my family. The fourth chapter describes my experience of liberation. In it I include my radically altered view of what family life can be and the new world of ideas that has now captured my mind, introducing me to experiences of which, as a child, I could not even dream.

Finally, in the fifth chapter, I have described the present outcome of my personal spiritual pilgrimage. This entire book is, in a sense, an account of my brief spiritual journey, even though I have chosen to limit the specifically religious dimension of my life to the last chapter. There have been times when I felt the absence of God as doubts came upon me, and I have had many questions. There have been other times when the presence of God has been so near that I felt I could touch him. I know that the only way I have been able to survive many of the experiences described in this book has been through his support and guidance. Through times of both doubt and assurance, I have developed a faith that has been sufficient to sustain me during the most difficult crises; and, therefore, I have been led to relate my story to others. Most of my readers have never lived in a truck, but all have their own problems. My hope is that my story may be of help in facing those problems.

I hereby express my deep-felt appreciation to Professor Elton Trueblood for his friendly reaction when I told him that I hoped to write my brief story. I am grateful to him not only for his personal encouragement, but also for giving me suggestions about literary style when I have needed them most. I am likewise grateful to my husband, James, for his suggestions and his patience when I have been writing instead of spending time with him, and to Evelyn Wicke and Mary Benson for their help in typing successive versions of the manuscript.

My relationship to my mother-in-law, Doris Newby, who has also helped with typing, and to my father-in-law, Richard Newby, and other members of the Newby family has been utterly different from anything I ever knew in my childhood. All of them have encouraged me to go on writing when I have been deeply discouraged. Others to whom I am indebted are Helen Chapin and Neil Snarr, professors at Wilmington College, for their assistance, and Debbie Overmyer at the University of Cincinnati for her help in editing.

ELIZABETH LOZA NEWBY

Cincinnati, Ohio

Contents

1
My Home on Wheels

Until I was fourteen years old, I was never conscious of sleeping anywhere except in the back of a truck. My father, unable to keep a steady job due to lack of education and comprehension of the English language, decided to take the advice of a close friend and join the migrant circuit in the spring of 1948, when I was sixteen months old. He invested all of his money in a 1942 Army surplus truck, which was to become our home for the next thirteen years. He cleaned and repaired the bed of the truck to make it suitable for living. Orange crates were used for stands and cupboards and baby beds (my first bed was an orange crate). An old-fashioned metal tub filled with coal was our stove, providing heat in cold weather.

As I outgrew my orange crate, my bed was transferred to the floor, where three or four hand-sewn quilts from Mexico provided me with a mattress. Since there were no partitions separating my parents from my brothers and me, we had to learn to get along together. Over the top of the truck my father fastened a tarpaulin, constructed to resemble the roof of a house in order to give us protection from the weather. Occasionally the tarpaulin would rip, and my father would have to repair it, using needle and thread. Along the side of the truck we carried two fifteen-gallon containers of water, since the places where we camped often had no fresh water supply. I can remember the sound of this water splashing from one side of the container to the other as our truck rocked us back and forth, transporting us from field to field in the slow-moving migrant caravan.

All in all, our truck served us well during those thirteen years on the road. Compared with the migrant housing provided by many of the farmers for whom we worked, ours was luxurious. As I grew older, I helped my mother keep the truck spotlessly clean; and, by camping away from the rest of the migrants, we escaped the epidemics of tuberculosis, influenza, measles, and other contagious diseases. For a young girl this kind of life was an adventure. Many of my school friends often crowded around me at lunchtime, wide-eyed and anxious, eager to listen to stories of our travels. I remember telling about the "wild animals" that would gather around our campfire at night and about how we went swimming in the irrigation ditches that surrounded the fields where we worked. Of course I exaggerated many of these stories as my friends listened with excitement, feeling that my unique style of living had brought me acceptance from my schoolmates.

I discovered later, however, that my uniqueness did

not really bring me acceptance, but only disappointment and hurt. Though for a while my classmates enjoyed my stories of our travels, these soon became boring. At each new school that I attended (I went to twenty-two different elementary schools), it wasn't long before I found myself alone—except for my family.

In the second grade, when I was seven years old, I had my first encounter with prejudice. In a small town in northwest Texas I had become very good friends with a little blue-eyed blonde named Kathy, who happened to be the daughter of the town mayor. Both of us were totally unaware of our differences of race and social class. She was the first real friend I had ever had, accepting me for what I was—a little girl the same age as herself. We ate our lunches together at school and talked about our families.

One day, as we were walking home together from school, I saw a tall man dressed in Western clothes, complete with boots and a ten-gallon hat, approaching us from a distance. As he drew near I could see the expression on his face, which portrayed anger. My little friend screamed "Daddy!" as he grabbed her arm and quickly walked with her the rest of the way to their home, leaving me standing motionless by the side of the road. I was so stunned by what had occurred that I could hardly wait until the next day to speak to her concerning this perplexing incident.

The next morning, when I stopped by the tree where we usually met so we could walk to school together,

Kathy was not there. Not wanting to be late, I hurried on to school without her. At recess, when I finally found her, she ignored me. Though I was deeply hurt by her actions, I persisted with my questions. "What happened yesterday? What's wrong?" Finally she broke down in tears and repeated to me what her father had told her, adding, "You have got to stop bothering me. My father told me that you are different, and I am not allowed to play with you anymore!"

Needless to say, I was stunned. Many questions that had never been there before came to my mind, and to this day I have a difficult time relating this incident without a gnawing in my stomach. As I slowly walked back to my schoolroom, the noise of the playground seemed deafening. I pondered the meaning of what my friend had told me. *What does it mean to be different?* I asked myself. I was confused and deeply hurt, and my life was changed because of what happened on a school yard in a small Texas town in the fall of 1954.

At this point Mrs. Freeman became a central figure in my life. She was my teacher when this first encounter with prejudice occurred. Mrs. Freeman was in her late thirties or early forties when she was my second-grade teacher. She was of average height with dark brown hair and the most beautiful green eyes. Not only were they beautiful in color, but they were also kind in expression. She always stood at the entrance to her room and greeted us as we returned from the playground.

As I approached the door after recess, she could tell from the troubled expression on my face that something disturbing had occurred while I was outside. Taking me by the hand, she questioned me about the nature of the problem confronting me. I related to her, from start to finish, my encounter with Kathy. She stared at me for a brief moment, trying to grasp a quick strength so that she could compose herself and convey to me, at the same time, a sorrowful message. As she spoke to me concerning this first encounter with prejudice, I could feel both the love and the hurt she was experiencing through her counseling. It was quite obvious that she was forewarning me of discriminating experiences to come. She explained about my differences, which were, she said, of genuine cultural value, partly because they added to the variety of life in our country. By the time she had finished talking with me, I felt that I was ready to meet whatever might come.

The most significant thing she said was this: "People, all people, fear the unknown." This became the guiding thought in my life whenever and wherever I encountered discrimination because of skin color or language. For me, Mrs. Freeman exemplified what is meant when we speak of "a concerned person." She helped me through this very difficult time, as she gave me both her love and a better understanding of my own background than my parents could have provided. From this time on I became more aware of my encounters with prejudice and discrimination. In every new school I attended, I was learning what it meant to be a Mexican migrant in the Southwest.

I recall very lovingly the day I told my mother of this

first encounter with discrimination. My mother is a loving, Christian woman whose beautiful face shows signs of struggle, hurt, and suffering; but with her bright black eyes, curly black hair, and handsome smile, she is still personally attractive. There seems to be a serenity about her, and this calmness in the face of the most adverse conditions soon gave me a model by which to live. As I related the disturbing incident of discrimination, my mother took me in her arms, hugged me, and reassured me of her love, which was just what I needed. What she said at that time has long been forgotten, but the sight of the tears that filled her big black eyes will remain with me forever. I could see the pain and hurt that she tried to conceal; and that night I could hear her softly crying, even though she tried to hide her feelings.

When thinking about our many travels, I remember vividly the experience of being caught in a huge snowstorm. We were on our way to our home base in southern Texas in 1957 when the storm hit. Dad carried extra equipment and food supplies for such emergencies. (We had had experience with a hurricane two years before, so he made better preparations for emergencies after that.) We had been traveling south, and my father thought that doing so would keep us out of the snow; but it did not. The blizzard kept getting worse, and before long we were among the many who were stranded. Dad parked the truck in a driveway leading to a cattle pasture, got out our old metal tub, and filled it with coal. Since we had the heat from the tub and plenty of blankets, we were able to survive throughout the first night.

The next morning we discovered that we were almost completely buried in snow. After Dad had managed to dig his way out, he shoveled off as much snow from around the truck as he could. He had hopes of getting the truck started and moving on; but after repeated attempts, he decided that the truck was not going to start. He concluded that we must just sit it out for the next couple of days.

After a few hours of our sitting and getting on one another's nerves, my father decided to venture out and explore the area. Not far from where we were parked, he found a farmhouse; and he helped the resident farmer to rescue what they could of his cattle. Then they both went to help others who were caught totally unprepared. All of us made it, for we shared with them and they shared with us. Dad earned enough money that day to get more food and supplies. We didn't find out until later that the farmer had offered him a job, which he turned down. When we did discover this, we were disappointed. By this time all of us were growing tired of the migrant life, with its constant uprooting and change of schools.

This was the first time that my brothers and I had experienced snow. We had great fun throwing snowballs at each other, running until we fell, exhausted, in huge snowdrifts. Since we did not have any winter clothing, Mom made us wear double of everything and refused to allow us to play outside for very long before making us get back in the truck to warm our snow-covered bodies by the fire in our metal tub.

During this snowstorm I discovered, for the first time in my young life, that, in a genuine crisis, no one seems to care about the race or nationality of the victims. In times of real danger everyone is willing to help everyone else to survive. How I wish we could all learn to help each other survive even when there is no crisis.

During all of our travels, regardless of where we were, my mother always made sure that my brothers and I went to school. Since we had little money, our school clothes were hardly more than rags. Mom had an old Singer pedal sewing machine, on which she remade some hand-me-downs. Sometimes she made us new clothes from flour sacks. Children were cruel and called us names because our clothes looked strange. Because of this name calling (such as "Flour-bag Pants," "Dirty Mexican," et cetera), my brothers were always getting into fights and were consequently expelled from school. This hurt my mother deeply because she wanted her children to have just as much knowledge as other children had. I remember her kneeling in the corner of our truck home, praying for her children and asking that they be released from the burdens that migrant life placed upon them.

I have been told that when I was two years old, Mother had another baby girl. She was a "blue baby," and Mother took her to doctor after doctor and clinic after clinic, hoping that someone would be able to give assistance. But after watching her baby suffer for nine months, she saw her die. Later Mother gave birth to an autistic boy, who is now living in a state hospital. In spite of these two very personal tragedies, my mother has been able to keep a strong Christian faith. Whereas another's faith might have faltered under the hardships that life brings, my mother's faith has grown deeper. She has told me many times about the strength she has received from prayer and about how God, the Great Comforter, has been able to provide help during difficult times. She has lived her faith and has consequently provided us with an example by which to live.

In the Latin culture, life centers around the male, who expects to be served; and, since I was the only girl in the family, a great deal of work was expected of me. For example, I was supposed to take care of my younger brothers and also to do all of the housework and preparation of meals, while the rest of the family worked in the fields. Because I hated to see Mom go to work in the fields all day, I tried to make life as easy for her at home as I possibly could. Always I arose early, started the fire, and cooked breakfast before anyone else was awake. Trying to keep up with my work at school, in addition to all that was expected of me at home, became a serious struggle. Early in life I naturally decided that I was determined not to live the life of a migrant forever!

I remember the time when Dad left us for about two months, though to this day I do not know why he went away; and I have never had the courage to ask him. Mom kept us moving with the circuit, but after two weeks she became worried, borrowed a car from a friend, and left us to look for our father. She feared that some disaster had overtaken him. We children were left alone for six weeks, during which time I took care of our home and my younger brothers, while a friend drove our truck in the caravan.

Being without our parents for that length of time, alone and frightened as we were, was like living in a bad dream. We were insecure enough without losing our parents, who provided the only security we had. I would stay up night after night waiting for them, fearful that they would never return. I used to imagine what it would be like if they never came back, as I was left in complete charge of my brothers and myself. The thought of such an awesome responsibility brought tears to my eyes, and feelings of hatred for my parents were difficult to avoid.

One late summer afternoon, as I was hanging some laundry out to dry, I saw a car fast approaching our truck home. I quickly jumped into the truck, closed and locked the door, and peered through a rip in the tarpaulin to see who it could be. As the car came closer, I recognized it as the one that my mother had borrowed to go and look for Dad. Upon even closer observation, I recognized my parents as the people in the car. My heart was in my throat, and tears filled my eyes as I opened the door and jumped from the truck to meet them. My brothers also saw them as they arrived at the door of our truck home. They came running from a nearby irrigation ditch where they had been playing. It was a joyous reunion, Mom and Dad having brought with them fresh meat and other food for a celebration meal. I was very thankful for their return; and, after this experience, I was prepared for just about any crisis that might arise.

For my family, each new day brought both new adventure and new problems. There was the time in Nebraska when, after we had finished hoeing several acres of sugar beets, the owner informed us that he wasn't pleased with our work. Rather than have us do it over, he simply refused to pay wages. My father tried to argue with this farmer, but without success. My mother stood back by the truck with her arm around me, her face filled with hopeful anticipation. When my father turned and walked away from the farmer empty-handed, my mother's face hardened. Without saying a word she lifted me up into the truck, and we began our journey to the next field of work.

Because we were not prepared for this man's refusal to pay us, we didn't know what to do when faced with such a situation. Of course we needed the money to buy food and supplies to keep moving, so this setback caused real hardships. Since my parents, along with other migrants, were and still are ignorant of their rights and laws designed to protect them, rather than trying to get help, we just moved on to the next job and prayed that this type of incident would not be repeated.

Economic injustice was one of the major types of discrimination that we encountered during our travels around America. Low wages or, at times, no wages for work done, high prices for commodities that we bought in large quantities, and inability to secure loans kept us in a cycle of poverty that was literally inescapable.

There are many government agencies set up to guard against violation of minimum-wage laws, but migrants do not have the know-how or enough comprehension of the English language to file complaints against those employers who are unfair to them. We never knew whether or how much we would get paid until we were ready to move on to the next job. Such was the life of our family, and such is the life of others who are still following the harvest circuit.

I suppose the most irritating of all economic injustices directed toward us was the raising of prices by local merchants on foods and supplies that we bought while we were working in the community. When I was sent to the store to buy a sack of flour, I was often told by the clerk that the price was higher than the thirty-nine cents marked on the package. Since we had to have food to survive, we always paid what the clerk said, regardless of the inequity. Some merchants were more clever, creating new price labels and placing them over the original price marks. We knew that this adjustment was not right; but since we were ignorant of our legal rights, we did not try to do anything about it. Part of the problem came about because we were in each community for such a short time that we just accepted what we were given—or not given—and moved on to the next place, trusting that the new situation would be different.

The Mexican migrant is in a constant cycle of economic exploitation. Powerful agricultural interests have been able to keep the migrant the most underpaid and the most oppressed worker in America so that these interests can continue to yield a surplus of cheap agricultural labor. This oppression in a land of plenty has caused me great sorrow. To witness the exploitation of my people, to have been used in this way, has left me saddened. When a whole group of people is seen just as cheap labor with little or no regard for their lives as children of God, I am tempted to become bitter. When the worth of an individual is measured by the number of rows he can hoe in an hour or the number of tomatoes he can pick in a day, then I weep for our nation and my people. Somehow we must recover the idea that people are not something to be used and then put aside, deported when they are no longer needed to do a job—only to be lured back into the poverty cycle when they are needed for the next year's harvest.

Some of the events that occurred during our travels were puzzling, partly because I wasn't sure whether or not they occurred intentionally. There was the time in Oklahoma when we were picking cotton. All of a sudden a crop-dusting plane descended upon the field in which we were working, spraying it with insecticides. Dad heard the plane coming and, having experienced this before, yelled to everyone to go to their vehicles and close the windows. Though most of them did, a few did not; and they soon became ill from exposure to the insecticide. I don't know whether the farmer failed to tell the pilot that there would be people in the fields or whether he just didn't care. At any rate, my people were needlessly exposed to harmful chemicals for reasons that we never knew or understood.

Most of the communities in which we settled maintained camps for the migrants. In all communities we soon discovered "our place" and knew that we were expected to stay there. The camps were usually in isolated areas, sometimes far out from town. Most camps provided no running water, electricity, or any kind of sanitary facilities. The camp buildings, usually oblong in shape, had doors at each end, but often lacked windows. Inside there were rooms divided by very thin walls. The camps were usually overrun by weeds, cockroaches, rats, mice, snakes, and whatever else could get into the camp buildings. Each migrant family was given one room, which was supposed to house anywhere from nine to twelve people. This room, being living room, bedroom, and kitchen, had no door; so if anyone wanted privacy, he usually put a sheet or blanket across the doorway. The buildings were similar to military barracks, but without windows.

As I said earlier, my parents never approved of living in such conditions; and Dad usually parked our truck a mile or so from the camp in order to keep us from contracting some of the diseases that usually hovered over these human cattle barns. Some farmers did try to improve some of the camps, but usually the buildings were so cheaply constructed that their efforts were doomed to failure. The farmer could usually reason that, since we didn't stay very long, it wasn't worthwhile to improve the buildings. *Besides,* he would think, *the migrants did not take care of them anyway, so why waste time and money in trying to fix them up?* There were no camps that were better than others. They were all the same—terrible!

Most of the communities in which we worked totally ignored us, except that the officials made sure we did not spend too much time in any one place. We were to do our job, then move on to our next job. If there was ever any trouble in the community, such as an incident of disturbing the peace, a burglary, or a murder, the first place the police visited was the migrant camp. Though sometimes migrants were responsible for the crimes committed, in many other instances they were not. Due to the lack of communication between English and Spanish-speaking people, many injustices took place. Some migrants who were charged with committing crimes could not understand, because of their lack of English, what they were being charged with. I soon discovered that migrants frequently received treatment very different from that given others who had been arrested for similar offenses. The migrant stood more of a chance of being roughed up by the police and was given harsher sentences than others, simply because he spoke in a different language and had a darker skin.

The Mexican migrant's attitude toward the law, the police, and the courts is one of distrust and hostility. Migrants know that the local community has, in them, a scapegoat for all of the burglaries, murders, and rapes that occur while they are in the area. What I soon observed was judicial punishment of men or women who did not even understand why they were arrested.

One of the really surprising features of our migrant life was that, in spite of my extreme youth, I was regularly recruited to translate for members of our crew who understood no English. Young as I was, language study was easy for me; and I was able to translate from English to Spanish while I was still a child. Consequently, I was often called to the local courthouse to help migrants understand why they were being arrested, then to interpret for them during the court hearing. This was a difficult job because neither the arrested person nor the child interpreter was a match for the surrounding power structure. We knew nothing about lawyers; and when one was appointed to defend the arrested Mexican, the trial was an uphill battle. The defendant had often been convicted, in the minds of the judge and jury, even before the trial had begun.

The stereotype of the "lazy, thieving, drunken Mexican" has even to this day persisted in the minds of many people; and the police, feeling frustrated at their inability to communicate with an arrested Mexican migrant, often use violence to penetrate the communication barrier. Officers sometimes feel that this action will "keep them in their place" and will show the other members of the migrant community what will happen if they "get out of line." If two men are disorderly in public, one a white businessman of the community and the other a Mexican migrant, the usual police reaction is to tell the businessman to go home, but to lock the other in jail.

What bothers me most is the discrepancy. Why should one be politely told to go home and the other one beaten and jailed? Equal justice under the law is a constitutional right, but it is one on which the Mexican migrant cannot always depend. We learned early in our migrant experience in this country that the police were people to fear instead of persons to whom we could go for help and protection. We soon discovered that the white man takes care of his own and that, if we are to survive in white society, we have to protect ourselves.

The Mexican migrant is, in many instances, kept in jail unnecessarily and for long periods of time because of deeds for which others would not even be jailed. In a court of law his case is not presented well because of his lack of legal assistance and the absence of an interpreter. It was truly pathetic that I, as a young girl, was considered an adequate interpreter. A man is sometimes imprisoned for nonpayment of fines simply because he does not have the money. Statistics might make Mexican migrants appear more delinquent than others; but migrants may only be more unfortunate or may lack resources and the education needed to help them to endure the arrest-conviction procedure.

How to change the system so that it is more equitable for all is a question that must be answered. We can no longer afford the luxury of justice for some, but not for all. We can no longer allow the dehumanization of a particular people just because they are ignorant of the laws and because they are unable to communicate in an unfamiliar language. We must work toward the time when the law will transcend the barriers of race and language and will provide protection and justice for *all* people.

During our thirteen years on the road, we never saw a doctor, a nurse, or anyone else who could or would give us medical aid. Many of my people died of illnesses such as influenza or pneumonia, which, if properly treated, would not have been fatal. There are migrant children and adults who have crippled or deformed arms and legs because when their bones were broken, they were never set properly or not set at all. Mothers died while giving birth and babies died at birth simply because of the absence of medical care.

Those who needed medical help usually went into the nearest community to seek it; but we soon found out that, without money or medical insurance (we didn't even know what insurance was), hospitals would not treat us except in cases of critical injury. To see friends suffer and be helpless to do anything about it hurt me, and there were times when I became bitter toward the white man because of the injustices done to my people. It wasn't hard to hate or become bitter, but I found it very hard to be forgiving, remembering what my second-grade teacher had said about people fearing the unknown. All we wanted was a chance to learn to live and hope for a future with promise.

In all of my migrant life, I never witnessed a truant officer visiting any of the migrant camps near which we lived. Many of the children were either left at the camp or taken to the fields. Left unattended while the parents were working, children were sometimes injured in accidents—cutting their feet with hoes, falling out of trees, and being run over by trucks driven down the rows of the field. Some developed terrible infections from stepping on rusty nails and old metal roofing in the camps. These children, of course, should have been in school, but compulsory attendance was not enforced. Parents, afraid of school, which meant progress and change, not to mention the lack of money for their children's school needs and clothes, deliberately discouraged attendance. Those who did attend were often placed in classes where they were the oldest, so they felt awkward and out of place. They didn't belong in a class their own age, since academically they were far behind; but in most cases the teacher had too many children in the class and was unable to give the migrant children the extra help they needed.

Because they move around so much, it was and still is difficult for migrant children to keep up with their proper classes. Since migrants were in each local community for only a short time, school officials decided not to get them involved in school. However, there have been many improvements in this situation during the last few years. Because of the support of federal funds, there are now migrant schools, which represent a real advance.

In the area of education, I was very fortunate during my elementary, junior, and senior high school days—partly because language came easy for me, and I loved the work. School opened up a whole new world for me, one that many migrant children never know. The importance of education was always downplayed by the migrant community because of the threat it posed to the existing order and because of the seemingly useless hours one had to spend behind a school desk when he could be out in the fields earning wages. Since the parents didn't care about education, it was very difficult to make the children care.

In addition to the difficulty of making migrant parents understand the importance of an education, migrant children are also faced with the barrier of discrimination. Though education is the key that unlocks many doors for the migrants and is the basic answer to our problems, in order for education to be helpful to us, we must not only make the migrant aware of his need for a better education, but also break through the discrimination barrier. Since the Mexican migrant child is raised in a Spanish-speaking home, he has a great deal of difficulty adjusting to a school situation where the instruction is in English. Not only must the Mexican migrant student learn the subject matter; he must also learn the language in which it is taught. The school system in many American communities is just not prepared to meet the needs of the Spanish-speaking students.

A direct result of the language problem has been the idea, put forth by many, that Mexican migrant children are less intelligent than are other children. This notion is, of course, false; but because of the difficulty in communication, the dummy stereotype of the Mexican migrant child has persisted. Many of the teachers I had would make the Mexican students sit in the back of the room. And, since they could not understand what was being taught, they were allowed to draw or play games while the teacher concentrated on the other pupils. Such segregation in the classroom was very embarrassing and contributed greatly to the feeling of inferiority that was already so much a part of our lives. The back of the room became the place where the dummies all sat, and this stigma caused both pain and resentment.

Another big problem that Mexican migrant children have to face is the constant moving from one community to the next, which makes a continuous education almost impossible to obtain. As I mentioned earlier, I attended twenty-two different elementary schools, and this number was about average for most of us. The conviction at most schools was that, since we were in the community for such a short time, adjusting the whole school program to meet the needs of the migrant children was not worth the trouble.

The problems that come with going to school and college are, for most migrant children, truly insoluble.

Most migrant children drop out of school and find menial jobs rather than trying to put up with the struggles of securing an education. Because of their inability to comprehend the English language, because they are segregated in the classroom and made to feel inferior, and also because they are constantly moved around, migrant children tend to get caught up in the same cycle of poverty that their parents have experienced. Education is the way out of this poverty cycle, but few are able to take advantage of all of the benefits that education can bring.

As I grew up in both the American and Mexican cultures, I was able to pick up the English language easily. Though Spanish was spoken at home and I was comfortable using Spanish with my family and friends, I knew that if I were to escape from the migrant life, I was going to have to master English. Since I viewed education as the most important thing in my life, I knew that I had to be able to speak and comprehend the language that was used at school. With the help of some very special teachers and an understanding mother, I was able to break the cycle that has imprisoned so many of my people.

My story, however, is the exception rather than the rule. Somehow education must be suited to fit the needs of all children—Mexican or white, rich or poor. The migrant child, even though he is a temporary resident of a community, even though his language is different, and even though his culture is looked upon as strange by most Americans, *must* be given a chance to succeed in school. Likewise, this statement means that integration must replace segregation in the classroom. Finally, it means that a school system must work with children where they are in their educational development, not where it would be desirable for them to be.

We are living in a world in which people are constantly crossing cultures. We are no longer isolated from each other as we once were before the automobile and the airplane. With this increase in travel, we are made aware of our shrinking world and the many different peoples who inhabit it. The education of Spanish-speaking children is part of the worldwide concern of building communities where people from different cultures can participate equally in working for the common welfare of all. Through migration, peoples of different origins, languages, and cultures are coming together. As migration is bound to increase, the problems of living together will become more difficult. These problems must be solved, not ignored, for the survival of our country and our world depends upon a solution.

My father is one of those migrant men who feel that education is not only a waste of time, but also a threat to his authority and the existing order of the home. He is a strong, mean, profane, prideful man. I cannot recall hearing a sentence come out of his mouth that did not contain a curse. He demands and receives respect from his migrant worker peers, and this has been true wherever we have traveled.

My father's dress is an aspect of his character that is

very important to him. His day-to-day outfit consists of khaki trousers and shirt, both perfectly ironed, with just the right amount of starch. He always wears a Stetson hat and boots, without which he feels he would lose his mark of identity. He is a handsome man, over six feet tall, with brown hair and hazel eyes (Spanish characteristics), and very white, even teeth. He always smells of strong after-shave lotion and Swisher Sweet cigars. I do not remember a time when he didn't smell good. Even now I can picture him coming to the breakfast table, putting his hat beside his plate, and eating Mother's great Spanish omelette with coffee and tortillas. He has done this every morning as far back as I can remember. Then, just as quickly as he has arrived, he rises from the table, puts on his hat, lights a cigar, and is on his way to the fields, leaving behind the sweet-smelling aroma of after-shave and cigar.

A recent photograph of him in a local paper shows him, in all his glory, in the midst of a group of migrant farm workers in a cantaloupe field. He has the big cigar in his mouth and the Stetson hat on his head and appears to be in command of the situation. He is actually keeping a record of the production of the other workers.

To my father, all of life is seen as a fight. He builds a wall around himself, which is really an invisible wall of protection. He was taught never to apologize or to show any signs of cowardice. One can almost see the invisible shield of protection with which he surrounds himself as he leaves home to go to the fields in the morning and as he bends and picks tomatoes, silently moving from one plant to another. His face is the face of silence, inwardness, and protection. He will bend, stoop, and humbly obey every command of his white master, but he will never back down; moreover, he will not allow his privacy to be penetrated by any outsider.

My father is an honorable man. He is constantly on guard, ready to repel any attack against his masculine honor. *Never back down* are the words that he lives by. I remember, with reluctance, the many times in my childhood when my father felt that his honor was in jeopardy. The anger that would swell his eyes and the arguments and fights that would result filled my childish mind with terror. I can never forget the time when we were all sitting in the living room (after we had moved to a house) and migrant men in a truck fired a gun through the front window as they passed us. The bullet holes are still in the walls—one is covered by a picture of the Virgin Mary, and the other one is behind a wall hanging of John and Robert Kennedy. For this act of violence directed toward his family, my father reacted by seeking the men out, then running them and their families out of town. I do not know what caused the shooting, but I can be fairly sure that the reason was that my father had challenged someone's pride.

My father is a man of deep convictions, whether they are right or wrong. He carries with him a deep commitment to tradition and the Mexican culture. There were and still are many things about him that I do not understand—such as why he is so afraid of change and progress. This problem may sound like one that is common to all of us, but my father's fierce commitment to tradition is different and has hurt him many times.

My brothers also suffered in the struggle between change and tradition, between the Mexican migrant culture and American culture; but because they are males, it did not affect them in the way that it affected me. I have only four brothers. (We were a small family in comparison with other migrant families due to Mother's small build, which affected her pregnancies. She had seven miscarriages.) One brother, Juan, as I mentioned earlier, is an autistic child. He is the second to the youngest and is at present cared for very well in a state institution. My fear is that when he becomes eighteen years old he will be sent back home. This situation may be a real setback for him because the home environment is so different from that of the state institution that he will probably have difficulty in making a satisfactory adjustment. My parents have too many problems to overcome right now—financial, emotional, and spiritual.

My oldest brother, Diego, has never been able to outgrow his dislike and distrust for the white man's world in spite of the fact that he has been in the military service and has worked with Anglos most of his life. The hurt of discrimination and poverty have made him both bitter and resentful; he just has not learned to get along with other races and people who represent other backgrounds. Never having learned to read or to write

English well, he has not been able, for the most part, to understand his teachers in school. He has never been able to adjust to a way of life different from ours; and, when thrust into the outside world, he cannot cope with it. Unprepared to deal with what he finds, he does not live a happy life.

My two other brothers, José and Roberto, are getting along fairly well by living at home. The youngest, Roberto, is still in school; and I am always encouraging him, from a distance, to keep going. I know that my mother gives him moral support, just as she did me. So far José and Diego have dropped out of school, but Roberto has a good chance of completing his courses. I pray for him and for all of my brothers; I know what they are suffering. I love them very much and want them to find a faith, as I have, that will help them to handle their problems.

Watching the world from the back of a truck was a very interesting experience for a young girl, but a very limited one. Our world, because of fear, ignorance, tradition, and different cultural background, was stifling. It never occurred to us that the world was so much bigger than we knew. My brothers have never really made the adjustment away from the migrant life, and even for me it has been a long, difficult struggle.

Looking back on those thirteen years of movement, I find myself wondering how we survived without the modern conveniences that I now have. Little things like getting a glass of water, cooking a meal, or producing a light required much more time and effort than they would have if we had lived in a house or had even stayed in the migrant camp buildings. Life was an adventure, but not the kind of adventure one has for two weeks, from which one goes back to living a normal life in the suburbs. We camped continuously, unable to return to a more comfortable life after a brief time in the wilderness. Day in and day out we moved along the highway in a long string of trucks and old cars, all filled with sun-dried, emotionless brown faces. This slow-moving migrant caravan shifted from field to field; and as a young girl, a part of this roving subculture, I accepted this fate, never knowing the comforts of a house until I was fourteen years old.

2
Settled Migrants

After traveling the migrant circuit for thirteen years, from Texas to the Dakotas and from Indiana to California, we were very tired of the constant moving. So, in August 1960, my father accepted a job as a hired hand from a farmer in a small southwestern Kansas community. As we had traveled the migrant circuit, we had worked for this farmer each year; and every time he had offered Dad a permanent job. The rest of us were very happy when the farmer's offer was finally accepted, but for our mother the new decision was an answer to prayer. We became settled migrants—which meant that, though we still worked as farm laborers in and around our community during the harvest season, we no longer traveled all over tne country during the rest of the year. Settlement meant that when harvesttime ended, we still had a job with this farmer and could stay in the same place all year round. Though it was not a complete break from the past, this change produced a vast improvement in our way of life.

Harold Webster, the farmer who employed my father, was a wonderful man who possessed unlimited patience and an equal amount of love and concern for his fellowman. The first time I encountered Harold, after we had become settled, was at the edge of a field of sugar beets, where he was pulling weeds and waiting for all of the migrants to arrive for the day's work. Since my father was now his year-round hired hand, we were the first to arrive; and as he gave instructions on what we were to do, I interpreted them to my father in Spanish. Harold was dressed in a plaid lumberjack shirt and denim overalls, with a ten-gallon hat on his head and a rather large protruding pot belly under his top pockets.

Though he was in his late forties or early fifties when we first started to work full-time for him, he still possessed a youthfulness about his character that kept him very active. His hands showed much wear, and his fingernails were chewed to the quick. He had a kind face and was very jolly. He laughed with all of the migrants, trying to pick up bits and pieces of the Spanish language. His broken Spanish, along with his Southern accent, produced a drawl that was highly comical. We loved his easygoing ways and manners, and he was always teasing us children and chasing us with garter snakes and rotten cantaloupes. He also brought us candy and pop, which we devoured in no time!

He had a pet crow named Sam and a huge black dog named Blackie, who were his constant companions.

Sam would always ride on Harold's shoulders, sticking his beak into Harold's pocket to search for corn, while Blackie ran along behind them. Sam, Blackie, and Harold made an inseparable threesome.

Bearing with us as we faced the newness of our settled life would have discouraged ordinary men, but Harold laughed and cried with us, helping us learn to live in a comparatively civilized fashion. Recognizing our ignorance and dealing with it, he never allowed us to think that our situation was hopeless.

Our new landlord had a lovely family. His daughter, Jane, taught me to drive an automobile and introduced me to my first magazine—*Look.* She taught me how to curl and style my hair and helped me learn many little things about being a woman. She also tutored me in my schoolwork, helping me refine my English. Her lessons concerning the simple social graces were helpful to a young girl who knew nothing about life in society, apart from her own family.

Jane came to be my best friend. She had blonde hair and brown eyes, which seemed unusual to me because I had always pictured blondes with blue or green eyes. She wasn't particularly attractive, and her right hand was deformed; but she was far from homely. She was quite slim, and her father used to tease her, calling her "Bird-legs." They had a close father-daughter relationship, something that I admired since I was never able to develop this same kind of relationship with my own father.

Jane talked a great deal about boys, but for as long as I can remember she was never asked out on a date during high school. I know that she felt much less inhibited at home and wasn't as conscious of her withered hand as she was at school. In a way we held much in common, for I could feel with her when she was called names and shunned by her classmates. In order to avoid creating more problems for her, since being seen with a Mexican was not the most popular thing one could do, I usually didn't seek her out while at school. If she wanted to see me, she would always have to make the first move.

Once in a while, when her parents let Jane drive to school, she would come and ask my parents if I could ride with her. My parents held her and her family in such high esteem that they never refused her requests except when she wanted me to go someplace other than school, such as a ball game, a movie, or a dance. They would not allow me to go to any of these places.

The most important thing I learned from Jane was about myself. I was almost fifteen then; and I was certainly curious about sex, though I had not developed the nerve to talk with anyone about it. Since my mother never once mentioned anything concerning this private area of life, I am thankful to Jane for providing me with the knowledge I needed on this important subject.

The saddest day of the year 1965 was the day when Jane graduated from high school. She was a year ahead of me and went away to college in Nebraska, so my last year in high school was a lonely time without her. Though we corresponded for a time, we soon lost contact. I knew from her letters that college life opened new doors for her and provided a social life different from the one she had known at home. She married a distinguished man, who now teaches at a large eastern university. I am very happy for Jane, and I thank her for helping me to broaden my horizons at a time in my life when I desperately needed a close friend.

Our landlord's wife, Cora, taught my mother and me how to make bread, shop for groceries, use a washing machine, decorate a home on a limited budget, can and freeze food, and much more. We were unlearned children trying to cross a culture gap as we adjusted our lives to a new and different environment.

Cora was a lovely woman and always dressed beautifully. She was a chiropractor by profession and really quite sophisticated for rural Kansas. She carried on her practice in her home, and Mother and I cleaned her office and home once each week. She showed much compassion toward us, especially to Mother. She was beside herself when Dad physically abused my mother, and I came to trust her implicitly every time Dad lost control of his temper and beat Mom. Cora always came running with her first-aid kit in hand, ready to treat my mother's wounds. I can still envision her as she shook her silver head of hair in disgust and as her skilled hands gently patched my mother's cuts and bruises.

I shall always be indebted to Cora for the love she freely gave to my family. In a world of indifference she stood out as one totally dedicated to Christ and the betterment of humankind. When I think of her I am reminded of these words from Matthew: "I was hungry and you gave me food, I was thirsty and you gave me drink, I was a stranger and you welcomed me, I was naked and you clothed me, I was sick and you visited me" (25:35–36, RSV).

Mike, Harold and Cora's son, was a tall young man with blond hair and brown eyes. Since he was older than I, he already led an active social life. To me he was the most handsome boy in the world. I had a crush on him and used to dream about his taking me out on a date. I knew from the look in his eyes that he had discovered how I felt toward him from the first time we met. He was flattered by my feelings and loved to tease me. My brothers were terrible about teasing me in front of him, saying things like "Elizabeth loves Mike!" Consequently, I became so flustered and angry that I would always retreat into my room when he came over to visit.

Mike worked with his father, though they didn't get along very well. Harold was always yelling at his son for staying out late at night or for not cutting his hair. In spite of his run-around nature, which his father deplored, Mike was kind enough to teach my brothers much of what they now know about agriculture. Just as Mike's sister took me under her wing, he did the same for my brothers.

Needless to say, Harold and his kind family civilized us as much as they were able, introducing us to a better style of living. The Websters represented, in my eyes, a genuine paradox. Even though the daughter was handicapped with a withered hand, she was more active than most people with two whole hands, doing everything without aid and never complaining about her disability. The son, Mike, was reputed to be a dummy in school in that he was not good academically; yet for my brothers, he was a wonderful friend. Harold never went to church, and he and Dad had many drinking parties, but he was always loving and compassionate with us. This never ceased to puzzle me, for here was a good man who was not held in high esteem by his churchgoing neighbors. I was beginning to discover that church attendance, however important it may be, is not an adequate measure of worth for any individual.

Harold not only gave Dad a job but also built us our first home on solid ground, constructing it on the inside of a huge barn. Now that I look back on this first home, it wasn't much; but to us at that time, it was a palace. This barn home was located in the center of nowhere; our nearest neighbor was almost five miles away, and we were a mile from the main county road. The barn housed the farmer's tractors and other equipment, as well as fertilizer and seed. The cement floor was cracked and had sugar beet plants and wheat growing between the cracks, where seed and fertilizer had spilled. The roof of our house, which was under the roof of the barn, was used chiefly for storing extra seed and fertilizer; but it also provided a home for mice and birds. During April and May there was much activity on our roof, since

baby mice and baby birds all new and noisy greeted us
with the sounds of spring.

Outside our barn home my father and Harold had
planted grass and some small trees, trying to make up
for the lack of any greenery around the immediate area.
Due to the shortage of trees on the flatlands, during
spring and summer we experienced terrible dust storms
that could darken the brightest day and make it appear
to be night. These dust storms were a menace to the
farmers since the heavy winds blew away the topsoil.
Our environment was very desolate, but I have beautiful memories of looking out my window and seeing
miles and miles of sugar beet fields and wheat fields
waving in the wind, appearing, at a distance, to be
green oceans.

The interior of our new home consisted of five
rooms—all just for us! We actually had a kitchen with
hot and cold running water, a stove, and a refrigerator.
Turning on the water faucets was pure fascination for us
kids, and I think our parents had as much fun as we
did. We never ceased to be amazed at how the water
could appear by our simply turning a little knob—such
magic!

What was just as fascinating was the toilet. We were
intrigued by this contraption, for we had never seen one
before we acquired our barn home. My parents had
always forbidden us to use public rest rooms. The only
ones they had seen were those in migrant camps, which
were, in fact, filthy, unsanitary, and dangerous. It was

extremely difficult for us to wait all day in school; we hurried home in the afternoons to relieve our systems. Another reason for our unfamiliarity with indoor toilets was the fact that during our migrant life we used the great outdoors, with its corn fields, wheat fields, and bushes. It is easy to imagine the plumbing problems we created for ourselves by our lack of knowledge concerning the use of a simple toilet.

Our barn home also had two bedrooms; and because of the space shortage and my responsibilities for my three younger brothers, I shared one of the bedrooms with them. The home was also wired for electricity. We were fascinated with this modern convenience and played with the light switch until it broke. Then there was the gas heater. We burned ourselves many times before we decided that its main use was keeping us warm in the winter and not keeping us occupied in the summer. This was certainly different from burning wood and coal in an old metal tub!

The most fascinating gadget in our new home was the telephone that Harold installed for our use, not knowing how little we knew about it. We were connected to a party line, and, before long, our distant neighbors who shared the party line with us were reporting us to the telephone company. It was really something for us to experience the sound of people talking through this magic device. Had the neighbors realized that none of us could understand much of what they were saying, they might have been more relaxed. Anyway, Harold also helped us to learn how to use the phone correctly.

All in all, we survived our first experiences in our first home on solid ground without many crises. Though there were times when we could justifiably have been evicted from our barn home, we were, nevertheless, fortunate to have such a wonderful friend in our landlord. Consequently, we loved this home and worked hard to take good care of it. To this day, in spite of its poor condition, this home carries with it, for me, a great deal of sentimental value. I had always wanted a home like everyone else, and my dream had finally come true. No one could ever make me believe that this home was just a shack or a rundown building. It was *my home*, and in it I received a taste of a different kind of life. For me, this home provided a new security; and I rejoiced in the realization that I should never have to live in the back of a truck again.

Along with this home came new responsibilities. Since Mom always worked with Dad, the keeping of the home and my three younger brothers was still my responsibility. But now I also had a garden to tend as well as the work of freezing and canning vegetables. Though this was a heavy load for a teenage girl still in school, I was so busy that I never really had much time to think about its being too much.

My three younger brothers were far from easy to manage. I can't begin to count the number of diapers I have changed. The boys were terrors, to be sure, scaring me with frogs and snakes and engaging in what they thought were cute tricks. But I love my brothers, and it hurts me to see how they have failed to find purpose in life. Together we had many wonderful adventures that have remained as memories. I remember that, because we had very few toys, we improvised with what would be considered junk by most people—old cans, bottles, boxes, lids, et cetera. These items made adequate dishes for tea parties, play grocery store, play house, and other imaginative games that children enjoy. We also played with old tractor tires, one of us rolling the tire while the other tried to cling to the inside. One of my brothers always helped me when it was my turn to guide the tire, since on one occasion the tire got away from me and rolled down the nearby field toward the irrigation ditch. One of my brothers was inside and screaming. I chased after the tire, but it was too late to prevent it from landing in the irrigation water and soaking my brother from head to foot.

Like many other children, we invariably did things we ought not to have done. There was the time when my oldest brother tried to teach one of my younger brothers to drive a tractor. My younger brother lost control of the tractor, smashed our washing machine, which sat on the back lawn, knocked down the clothesline, and crushed one of our newly planted trees before my oldest brother was able to climb aboard and stop the tractor from careening into the field. My younger brother was taken from the vehicle somewhat shaken but relatively undisturbed by the excitement of his joyride.

Because we were left alone so much of the time while

both of my parents worked in the fields, we found
many forms of mischief to pursue and had a lot of fun.
There were times when anger would erupt between us,
punches and kicks would be exchanged, and feelings
would be hurt. But in spite of all of the bickering between brothers and sister, we could always unite during
a family crisis, such as when Dad would come home
drunk or leave home for days, never telling us where he
was going. During these particular times of difficulty we
truly experienced the meaning of a close brothers-sister
relationship.

As time passed, Dad began to get restless. Desiring a
few acres of his own, he finally managed to rent, from a
retired farmer in the same community, a small farm
without a house on it. The farmland, which was for-
merly pastureland, was very poor; but my father managed to get a loan from a friend and purchased some
used farm equipment so he could prepare the land for
crops. He worked and worked on this small farm and
loved every minute of his toil. In 1963 we had to rent a
home in town and leave my beloved first home, which
had meant so much to me. By 1966 Dad had done very
well with this small farm, for he has a genuine love for
the earth and a "green thumb."

The farmer who rented the land to Dad was impressed and told him that he would sell him the land if
his son-in-law did not want it. His son-in-law, who
already had plenty of crop land and was a big cattle
rancher besides, told the farmer that he did not want it,

thus clearing the way for my father to make the exciting purchase. In 1967 Dad was granted a loan from the government to buy the farm, little suspecting that 1968 would bring disaster.

First of all, the workers for the Colorado sugar company, with whom my father was doing business, went on strike, causing the company to refuse trainloads of sugar beets, my father's principal crop. Many farmers, Dad included, were unable to sell their sugar beets, thus experiencing a big loss. Dad was depressed and worried, but he found comfort in the fact that the government would help him. At this time, however, some of the federal funds allocated for small farmers were cut off. As a result, Dad, unable to get the money he needed to run his small farm for another year, lost it. This was a tragedy for the whole family, for it left us without anything. We were able to survive only because Dad secured custom work from the farmers in our community.

During all of this time, we had many "first" experiences. In 1963, on November 8, my birthday, we purchased our first television set, a used one that my father bought from our farmer boss. All of us were fascinated by television and just loved to watch it. We usually had to watch the shows my parents wanted to watch, such as *Bonanza*, *The Tall Man*, *Maverick*, and *Shane*. We hardly ever saw a variety show or a comedy. Both of my parents watched the afternoon soap operas when they were not working and became deeply involved in the lives of the make-believe characters, worrying if Johnny would divorce Linda or if Max would kill Sam for stealing his wife. The programs I enjoyed the most were the old movies that came on after the news, but I never really became a TV fan.

During this time of TV mania in my family, my love for reading increased. Since neither of my parents could read much English, they always inquired about the books I brought home from school. Often my parents did not approve of my selections and thus made me return them to the library. After having this happen to me a few times, I decided not to tell so much about them. If I felt that my parents wouldn't approve, I told them only what they wanted to hear.

The year 1964 brought me a new beginning. It was the year when federal programs for underprivileged people were initiated in my home community. It was the beginning of Headstart and other government programs designed to help children who would otherwise not be given an opportunity to leave home for a while and get at least one square meal a day. Money was also provided by the government for migrant health clinics, as well as for migrant adult education programs to help migrants read and write English.

My parents, like many others, were skeptical about all of these new programs. Only through the patient guidance of some government volunteers did my parents come to realize their need for learning if they were to read and write better English. My mother enrolled in a few English classes and has since kept up her reading so that she now speaks English reasonably well. Unfortunately, my father never took advantage of these opportunities, learning most of his English on the street.

1964 was also the year I stopped working summers in the fields and got a new job working for the county health nurse. She was a large maiden lady at least five feet, ten inches tall and weighing around one hundred fifty pounds. She was the very picture of what I had suspected a nurse would look like, all dressed in white and wearing a little white hat atop her head. I took her to all the migrant camps around the community, where she helped many of my people who were in need of medical attention. She vaccinated against infectious diseases, wrapped wounds, and set broken bones. I also accompanied the Headstart officials to the camps, and they were able to take many migrant children out of the fields and place them in the classrooms.

I was grateful for all of the new and wonderful opportunities that were at last being made available to my people, and I was glad to be a modest part of a new development. But because of their suspicious nature, it was difficult to get my people to understand their medical and social needs. They did not want handouts because accepting help would show that they were incapable of providing for themselves. Pride, which was and is a dominant characteristic among my people, often stood in the way of progress.

Not only did their pride cause them problems, but so did I. They were suspicious and cautious of me because

I was stepping out of the stereotyped image of a migrant girl. In a way I lost out on both ends—my people thought of me as having sold out to the Anglos, and I was the token minority for the white man's government. These images made my job very difficult. However, as the medical aid and migrant programs continued, more and more migrants began to make use of them; and they also began to trust me. The results of all these programs were slow, but I am proud to say that I am a product of the federal programs which the era of the sixties brought to my home community.

Though the summer of 1964 was a profitable and successful time for me, my home life was not improving. My parents fought constantly, sometimes becoming violent. My oldest brother was always getting into trouble with the law; my father was drinking heavily; and my mother was having a great deal of difficulty holding the family together.

In my family my brothers, as is customary in our Latin culture, were seen as more important simply because they were male. My parents believed that it was fine for my brothers to do as they pleased, with some minor limitations, while I was treated very strictly. I have always felt that my brothers were allowed too much freedom too soon. Too much permissiveness created many problems for both them and my parents. For instance, my father purchased an automobile for Diego, my oldest brother, as soon as he received his driver's license at age sixteen. Diego's abuse of this privilege cost my parents several traffic tickets, a wrecked car, and the heartache of having to bail their son out of jail because he was arrested for drinking while driving. He was much too immature for the freedoms and privileges that were allowed him at such an early age.

Also at age sixteen Diego began drinking heavily, got married (and eventually divorced), and proceeded to go against the law by his reckless and brawling nature. By my parents' bailing him out of trouble constantly, he never learned responsibility—only more dependency. It was not long before he had drained my parents both financially and emotionally. After several difficult years he joined the Armed Forces, where he is today. He is basically the same in nature, as this tendency toward rowdiness was established in him at an early age, except that now he depends on the Armed Forces for his security. I see in him, I am sorry to say, the replica of my father.

During all of the difficult trials that my father has had to endure, many of his feelings and thoughts have remained hidden. His relationships with other men are always coated with suspicion. Because of this distrust, he does not confide in others when there is even the slightest threat that the confidence will be betrayed or that the consequence will be dishonor. My father has never had any close friends, for to become really close to another would have threatened his privacy. His relationships are always surface relationships, such as that between worker and employer or worker and fellow worker. Even within the home he cannot let down this protection and become *himself*, open and vulnerable. To do so would be to surrender his manhood.

This suspicious nature, characteristic of the Mexican migrant man, has caused a number of violent arguments simply because incidents have been misinterpreted. To the migrant man, everything has another side. One is not nice to another just to be nice; each is obviously after something. One does not accept a gift from another because all that is wanted is something else in return. Suspicion, constant suspicion, was a part of my early life. When I said that I was going to the store, my brothers followed me to make sure that going to the store was all I had in mind. When I wanted to do something and confronted my father with my reasons, I was always questioned, always humiliated, and always made to feel that I was on trial at the witness stand. And in this I was not alone, for such is every Mexican migrant's life. Suspicion of everyone and everything kept defenses up so that the protective wall of privacy could not be penetrated.

Distrust of the white man is another common characteristic of the Mexican migrant male. This distrust has roots that extend back to the 1830s and 1840s, when the United States planned territorial, economic, and political expansion to the detriment of the Spanish people in America. The naturally suspicious nature of the Mexican has made distrust of the white man easy, but the long string of broken promises to my people has had an added effect. These include, as I mentioned earlier, the nonpayment for jobs that we did, just because the white farmer did not consider them done well; the shrewd business tactics of local white merchants that caused prices to jump on commodities that we bought in huge quantities; the name calling and the making fun of our way of life; the embarrassment of being told in a store that Mexicans are not welcome. All of this has turned the Mexican migrant community away from the white community, which, it is widely believed, is not trustworthy.

The Mexican migrant always tries to avoid a direct confrontation with the white community. If he keeps his place, goes to work, and returns to the camp at night, he is safe. If he dares to venture out of this rut, he cannot be sure of himself, for his shell may prove to be vulnerable to white attack. As long as the migrant man does the job he is expected to do and does not become a public nuisance by taking his family to a downtown restaurant or to Sunday church services, he is relatively secure. The moment he violates the community's mores by mixing with the white population, he can expect trouble from the police or violence from groups of white vigilantes.

When there are two cultures coming together, with differences in speech, eating habits, music, art, et cetera, and there is a feeling of distrust between people and a lack of sensitivity toward each other's culture, what happens? My personal observation has been that there is a growing inwardness of the minority, isolating them even more from the dominant culture, until the minority cannot take the subservient role any longer. Their frustration erupts in violence, both among themselves and against the white community. The acts of violence do not erupt in any organized way among Mexican migrants—at least not yet—but there have been individuals, bred in poverty and given second-class citizenship, who cannot take the humiliation any longer and who consequently express their feelings in violent acts. Because of the Mexican migrant's suspicious nature and the white man's prejudice, assimilation has been difficult.

The Mexican migrant man is taught never to back down, never to show any sign of emotion; and he looks upon those who do back down as cowards. Emotion is a sign of weakness, and weakness is the last thing he wants to show. It would be out of character for my father to show his true feelings all of the time; but just because his feelings remain hidden, it would be a mistake to assume that he has not been affected by everything that has occurred in his family. He cannot hide his eyes, for they express what he cannot say or allow himself to show. He has suffered a thousand deaths. My mother, by contrast, relied upon God for reassurance and comfort in a life of uncertainty, discomfort, and physical abuse. Her strength has been the binding force in our home, and her love has left its impression upon my life.

When my father would come into the house in a

drunken rage, Mother would always send us to bed or out to do chores. There were many times when, in this drunken rage, Dad would beat my mother. I remember lying in bed and hearing her scream and cry in pain as she was slapped and kicked. I would cringe in fear and feel for her as I yelled to my father, begging him to stop. Unfortunately, my mother still suffers from this physical abuse.

My father looks upon my mother as an instrument of his masculine desires. He places her on a pedestal and forces her to be the symbol of everything he is not—tender, religious (regular attender of a church), sensitive, and stable in a life of instability. He will not allow any disrespect to be shown to her from outside the home and reacts violently when someone damages the image that he has created for her. My father's attitude toward my mother is not peculiar to him alone. I have found this attitude to be true of migrant men in general and a trait of the Mexican migrant subculture.

The fact that I lived in a home where a woman was used in this way and that this home was part of a larger society that allows women much more freedom caused many arguments between father and daughter, mother and father, and brothers and sister. The Mexican idea that women are frail creatures who need constant masculine protection resulted in very little freedom and even less privacy. I view the respect we receive and the pedestal on which we are placed as a way of keeping us from expressing our true selves and thus becoming complete human beings—people with thoughts, feelings, and desires of our own. This was a constant struggle in my family, and my desires, such as wanting to go to college and to step out of my prescribed role, caused many family arguments.

Because women are seen as objects, as instruments of masculine desires, they are taught to remain docile when they are approached as sexual partners. Many women were raped in our migrant camps, and there was even some incest. The only girls who could remain virgins in this situation were the ones who could outrun both their brothers and their neighbors. Sexual liberties were taken by many, and nothing was done about it because women were taught to believe that they were less than human, not able to express themselves, and existing only because males need sexual satisfaction.

I recall an occasion when my uncle was visiting with us, and he chased me around the house when my parents were not there. He had been drinking and, as a result, became vulgar in both speech and actions. Luckily, my girl friend came by before anything serious happened. After this experience, I always tried to leave with my parents or sneak out on my own when the situation appeared conducive to attack.

It was a long time before I could even get close to a man. Living this way, always unsure of a man's intentions and always fearful of attack, caused me to seek professional help from counselors and teachers. They told me of ways to avoid rape and helped me develop ways in which I could have a meaningful relationship with a man without being afraid. Because of this much-needed help and counsel, I have been able to marry and live a happy home life with a man whom I truly love and trust absolutely.

Unfortunately, many women in the migrant camps were not as lucky as I was. Sexual abuse is a major social problem that can be stopped in the Mexican migrant culture only through a new understanding of what it means to be a woman. The idea that we are placed on a pedestal, the symbol of everything the male is not; the idea that women are placed on this earth to be used as sexual instruments at the whims of the male; the idea that a woman is vulnerable and frail, open for attack and fair game if she cannot defend herself—all of these must change! We must somehow learn to recognize that we are all children of God, worthy of fair treatment and of equal opportunity, love, understanding, and respect.

I do not mean respect in the same sense that it has been used in the past, but in the sense that women are recognized as individuals with feelings and desires that can be expressed without the guise of masculine protection hovering over them and smothering them. Women need to be respected simply because they are human beings; and they deserve it, not because they are seen as fragile and frail, unable to express themselves as persons, but because they are persons, valuable in God's eyes.

What Mexican migrant women symbolize in the white community is another concern. For some reason we are thought of as "easy." Many fights have been caused by white men's calling Mexican women sluts and whores. Obviously, this is at least disrespectful;

and if there is one thing the Mexican migrant cannot stand, it is the showing of disrespect toward *his* women.

I can remember that the white boys in school tried to take liberties with Mexican migrant girls, many of whom would submit simply because of the way in which they had been taught to think of themselves. This was very sad. Many girls, because of their poverty, sell themselves so that they can help put food on their family's table. Sometimes the parents know what is going on, though most of the time they do not.

In my girlhood I was immensely bothered by the way the white males looked down on us. To prove their masculinity they would often start stories about me that were untrue; the reward was congratulations from their peers. No boy could even get close to me because of my chaperoning brothers, but no one who heard the stories believed that. Many of these stories reached my brothers, and they would quickly stop the rumors by beating up the boy who started them. When, on occasion, a story would reach my father, he would always believe the rumor and punish me accordingly. This was difficult for me to understand. How could a father accept a rumor as truth, even when his own daughter was the subject of the rumor, and believe the rumor over her objections and tears? I think part of the answer has to do with his view of women.

Because the Mexican migrant woman is looked upon as the keeper of morals and the stabilizing force in the marriage, her natural job is the running of the home. She is the one who prepares the meals, raises the children, and pays the bills. She is the one who comforts her children when there is a problem at school and who puts them to bed at night. In the eyes of the Mexican migrant man, all of these tasks are considered women's work. The man's only responsibility toward the home is to bring in a paycheck; anything more is above and beyond the call of duty.

This Mexican migrant male attitude toward women appears to be close to the American male's attitude. Perhaps the chief difference is that, in the migrant farm worker's family, the woman is expected to do all of the housework plus share the work in the field. The home problems can be compounded when a woman returns from working all day in the field and is then expected to cook dinner, clean house, get the children ready for bed, and be a kind and loving wife. This arrangement does not make for a well-run home or a happy marriage.

Any occasion that enables the Mexican migrant to stop the routine of life and take time out to commemorate events and people is a joyful, wonderful happening. The big day of the year comes on September 15, when we celebrate Mexico's independence. In my childhood we started the day's activities by killing a cow or a pig, then preparing it and roasting it in an open pit. Throughout the day people made masks and clothes to be worn during the evening. We had modern as well as traditional folk dancing from our native land. There were beauty contests, which were not really based on

beauty but upon the number of tickets a girl could sell
for the evening dances. This gave every young lady a
chance to be a winner, regardless of appearance. (This
activity was always a disappointment for me because
my parents would never let me participate.)

Along with the so-called beauty contest there were
dancing contests, where the couple who could do the
best and most traditional dances would win prizes. In
these festivities the costumes played a major part, and
they were always beautifully made.

Christmas is also a big celebration, as it is for the
American people. We have mixed the Mexican with the
American tradition; the only difference is that we begin
our celebration about the middle of December and continue it until the middle of January. The big event in this
period is the breaking of the piñata, a papier-mâché
figure filled with toys and candies for the children, each
being blindfolded and given a bat with which to try and
break the piñata. When it breaks, all the children
scramble for the contents. The piñata, it should be
added, is used in many of our celebrations and is not
just limited to Christmas time.

These are just two examples of our times of celebration, and there are many, many more. The Mexican
migrant looks for any excuse to open a bottle of tequila
and thereby lose himself in a pleasurable experience.
During these fiestas we open up; we shout; we sing; we
shoot off fireworks. A holiday is a time of letting loose, a
time when all of the struggles of existence and all of the
frustrations of life are forgotten. For a few hours or days

we are free to do as we please—free to become drunk with the noise of loud music, joyful shouting, and color-ful costumes. We are able to explode and free ourselves from our subservient role.

In the celebration of a fiesta we are revolting from the way in which we are forced to live. Fiesta is a rebellion from the daily struggles that we must go through in order to earn food and shelter. During a fiesta the pride of my people becomes plainly visible, for we become more truly ourselves when we celebrate, allowing the closed wall of inwardness to drop and let our true feel-ings emerge.

Finally, the fiesta, our time of escape from reality, must come to an end. Too often it comes to a violent end, with someone in the camp getting shot or stabbed over a woman or someone's honor. This violence is equally a part of the celebration; indeed, it is almost a ritual. Whenever there are a number of closed, inward people coming together to open up in a time of celebra-tion, violence is always a possibility. As defenses are let down and persons become immersed in the joy of a fiesta, the tension mounts with each passing hour. Soon the freedom of a fiesta extends too far, causing someone harm, and violence erupts as a consequence. This oc-currence always brings a festive occasion back to the reality we are trying to escape. But since violence is a part of our culture, it naturally enters even our joyous occasions.

The extremes of life for the Mexican migrant have always interested me. The silence of the man and woman picking tomatoes and cantaloupes during the day, and then their release in the joy and splendor of a fiesta at night, followed by their sinking back into the closed wall of protection immediately following the celebration, seem remarkable. At one moment the migrant is totally subdued in the silence of daily routine, in his task of making a living; and the next moment his struggles and frustrations in life are forgotten. But just as quickly as a fiesta begins, it comes to an end. Life in all its drudgery beckons the migrant to return.

My times of celebration were severely limited during high school because the protective shell of privacy that encircled my parents extended to me, their only daughter. School was the center of my existence, my escape from my miserable home life. I loved school and accepted its academic challenges; but I was also disappointed that I was not allowed to develop equally the social side of my life. I was never allowed to take part in any school activities if participation required staying after school. I was not permitted to have any telephone calls from my peers, nor to go to the local drive-in for a soft drink or to visit with friends. Though at one point we lived directly across from the local theater, I was never permitted to see movies either alone or with friends. Consequently, I saw only three motion pictures before I left home, and my brothers chaperoned me each time. School was all I had, and I looked forward to it every day. Little did I realize, at the close of my sophomore year in high school, that even this enjoyment was threatened.

3

The Experience of Disownment

At the end of my sophomore year in high school my father decided that my education should be terminated. He thought that school filled me with too many foolish ideas, such as going to college; and besides, school was too worldly. My mother, on the other hand, always encouraged me to continue my education and was happy that I had stayed, but she hardly ever opposed Dad's wishes. He was the ruler of the home, and he made sure that we knew that. He did not see the need for me to continue my education: He had arranged a marriage for me when I was a child, and schooling was not necessary for me to be a wife and mother. I had known of this arrangement for a long time, for my parents had talked of it incessantly after my fifteenth birthday. Of course, this marriage arrangement custom was and is very old and is hardly ever practiced anymore. But since my father was very "old country," he saw nothing wrong with this ancient custom.

The young man whose wife I was supposed to become was about twenty-eight years old. He came from a very old French and Spanish family of our native home in Mexico. The first time I saw him was on a rainy spring afternoon when I arrived home from school. As I opened the door to our home, I was greeted by five smiling brown faces. I wanted to turn and run away, for somehow I could sense what was going to happen. The five people in the room were my mother and father, Pablo Rodriguez (the man I was to marry), and his mother and father. The Rodriguezes had traveled all the way from Mexico City to meet me and to take me back with them so that I could marry Pablo.

Pablo was a lawyer and looked forward to a bright career. He was about five feet eight inches tall, with brown hair and eyes. He had a small, stout build and wore a thin mustache. He was very courteous to me when I entered the room, standing and saying, *"Mucho gusto en conocerla, señorita"* (which meant "It is my pleasure to meet you, young lady"). I could tell that the arranged marriage seemed pleasing to him and his parents, but I did not share their opinion.

I was almost sixteen years old. I had had enough education and had developed enough determination to oppose my parents' wishes. After I was introduced and following the exchange of greetings, I immediately let my negative feelings concerning this arranged marriage be known to all in the room. I reminded them that this was not Old Mexico and that I should be allowed to have some judgment of my own concerning the choice of a marriage partner. I was determined not to be forced into a marriage I did not desire just for the sake of tradition. Consequently, I objected and refused to marry the chosen young man.

This action brought shame and disgrace to my father, and it was not to be forgotten. He tried to apologize to the Rodriguezes, but it was too late. They left as quickly as they had arrived, and my parents never heard from them again. My mother accepted my decision not to marry this man and assured me that Dad would overcome his feelings; but to this day, he has never forgiven me for refusing to follow his command in this matter.

It is easy to see how difficult it was for me to get my father's permission to continue my education after what had occurred. Once again, I called on one of my teachers for counsel regarding my educational dilemma. Mrs. Gilmore, the teacher to whom I presented my problem, had been very good to me throughout my freshman and sophomore years in high school. I could always count on her for guidance, since she was understanding of my Mexican migrant background and knew about my father's "old country" ways. I found her in her office at school, leaning over her desk and grading papers. When I knocked on her open door she looked up, startled, then sat back in her chair and invited me to come in and have a seat.

Mrs. Gilmore was in her mid-thirties, of average height and weight, with short, black hair. When I explained to her that my father was refusing to let me complete high school, she was enraged. Her bright blue eyes flashed as she removed her glasses and searched with me for answers to my dilemma. Never before had she been confronted with this kind of problem. Following a time of searching and consolation, she advised me to go to Mr. Mullen, the school counselor. After briefly telling him my problem over the phone, she made arrangements for me to see him immediately.

When I arrived at the counselor's office, Mr. Mullen had my file on his desk and was going over my grades. He asked me to be seated. Following a few moments of silence as he studied my file, he leaned back in his chair and said, "Elizabeth, I believe it is possible for you to graduate next year if you can obtain your father's consent to continue in school. This offer is dependent upon two considerations: First of all, you must maintain an average of C or better; and secondly, you must have a better attendance record."

The first stipulation didn't bother me, but I worried about attendance. My parents had always kept me home from school whenever they needed me for baby-sitting, housework, or work in the fields. I knew that even if I did get permission to continue in school, regular attendance was going to be very difficult. I thanked Mr. Mullen for his help and left for home in a perplexed mood. I was happy about the possibility of graduating the next year, but I worried about obtaining my father's permission.

I told my mother the good news, and she was very pleased. She said she would try to help me convince Dad to let me finish school. Time was of the essence; if I were allowed to finish high school, I would have to work and earn some money for clothes and other school expenses. I had decided to ask Dad the big question that evening, and until he arrived home from work I stayed in my room and practiced on how I might approach him.

Finally, after supper, I decided to ask him my pressing question. My whole body was shaking and my voice quivered as I explained to him the possibility of my graduating from high school the next year, if only he would allow me to go. Afterward there was a long silence. My father then said, "You do have your nerve! After all the shame you have put me through these past few months, do you believe that you can still do whatever you want?" Mom and I sat in silence, afraid to respond.

I then decided that I had nothing to lose by my insistence; so I started to tell him of the magnificent opportunity I was being offered, which did not occur often enough for our people. I was surprised at myself, and my mother and brothers sat in disbelief as they listened to my bold speech. Talking back to one's father in our culture was just not done, and by so doing I was risking severe punishment. My father became very angry, stood up from the dinner table, smashed his half-smoked cigar in his plate, and slapped me across the face. He sent me to my room crying.

My dear mother settled him down, and the next day she assured me that I would be allowed to finish school. She said that my father had been reluctant to give his permission; but late that evening, following a convincing argument by my mother, he had consented. She also said that she was counting on me not to disappoint her. I hugged her and told her not to worry. We then began to make plans for the completion of my last year in high school, sharing a mood of great happiness.

The last year of high school went by quickly. The work load was tremendous; the pressures were great; and my work at home was heavy. Often I stayed up late studying and got up early to do my chores before I left for school. Such was my routine, day in and day out. Mother did all she could to lighten my load, but I knew she couldn't do more. Besides, I did not want her to overwork.

My teachers were, for the most part, understanding. They had been familiar with my home situation over the years and knew that I was doing the best I could. Though I received no special treatment, I could feel their encouragement. When I would see a teacher in the school hallway, he or she would invariably ask, "How is it going, Elizabeth?" or say something like, "Keep up the good work, Elizabeth. All of us here at the school are pushing for you. I know you won't let us down."

I took one day at a time; and finally, at the end of the year, I received my high school diploma. Tears were flowing from my eyes as I walked down the center aisle in the school gymnasium and proudly accepted my diploma from the school principal. It was a joyous occasion, and I can still remember the proud expression on my mother's face as she snapped one picture after another with a camera she had borrowed from a neighbor. When we arrived home after the ceremony, I unrolled my diploma and read to Mother these wonderful words: "This certifies that Elizabeth Loza, having completed the course of study prescribed by the Board of Education of Unified School District 380, is therefore entitled to this Diploma."

It was a grand day of celebration; but even though it was a day to remember and the most exciting event that had ever happened to me up to that time, a more profound, life-changing event was about to occur.

Late one afternoon, within a week following my graduation from high school, Mother greeted me at the door to our home. I had been to the grocery store; and while I was gone, the mail had been delivered. My mother was holding a letter that was addressed to me from the school principal. She anxiously handed me the letter and asked me to open it immediately. I was nervous and scared as I ripped open the envelope, expecting to read the crushing news that there had been a mixup in their records and that, for some reason, they were rescinding my diploma. As I read the letter I discovered that I could not have been further from the truth. The note said that I was the recipient of a one-thousand-dollar scholarship for college.

The feeling that I experienced at that moment is indescribable. This was an impossible dream come true—an answer to prayer. At last I was being given the opportunity to escape from my dreary migrant existence.

While most of my classmates were destined to go to

institutions of higher learning, I considered myself fortunate just to complete high school. My sense of accomplishment, which my mother shared, is beyond expression in words. For Mother it was a wonderful experience to see one of her children graduate from high school, let alone have an opportunity to continue study in college. We were both ecstatic! The only thought that saddened our happy moment was the question of how we were going to inform my father about my opportunity to attend college. This sounds strange, since college is generally the accepted step after high school; but for me the opportunity turned out to be a major crisis and a very traumatic experience.

After all the excitement had died down, Mom and I began to think of a way to let Dad know of my chance for further education. Finding the right moment to tell him was going to be most difficult. Since the grant was good at any school I might choose, Mom and I decided to select an institution near relatives, where I could get help in obtaining employment or perhaps even stay with them while in college. After much consideration we decided on a college in southern Texas, where we had many relatives. We sent for an application and entrance papers and made all the arrangements.

We knew it was going to be difficult to tell Dad; but at this point I felt that I was in so much trouble with Dad from our previous problems that one more defiant act on my part would not make me any less endearing. We could not put off telling him much longer, since I was to leave in two weeks, but choosing the right moment was very important. Feeling that the right time had arrived, we finally told him.

To say that the roof came off the house is being half-truthful—it was much worse. He was furious! He was, in fact, so upset that he could hardly speak. The first thing he said was: "I knew I should never have let you go to school this last year. I have been too free with you, and all I have received in return is disgrace!" All this was beyond me, for I failed to see how going to college could be rebellious or disgraceful; and I pointed this out to him. Nevertheless, he continued his tirade and gave me the longest lecture I had ever heard on the evils of college and the terrible nature of career women. It seemed as though he would never finish. Mom and I sat in grave silence until his tirade ended. At this point we tried to tell him about the advantages of higher education and how I would be under the careful eye of relatives while I was in college. This argument did not help, and he stormed out the door while we stood there helpless.

He was deeply hurt, convinced that I had once again shamefully disobeyed him. He could not understand why I could not accept the traditional life-style of the typical Mexican migrant girl. I know that he loved me, but he just could not understand the changing times and felt threatened by higher education. I knew at this point that I could never be close to my father again, and this knowledge saddened me. But I could not turn back now.

Dad did not speak to me for the rest of the week. The

following Sunday, the day before I was supposed to leave, he finally approached me. My heart was in my throat, for I wanted him to be happy for me and to try to understand my decision. I suppose I was naïve to hope that he would change overnight, but my whole life had revolved around hope. This time, however, *I had hoped for too much.*

My father informed me that he had been doing a lot of pondering on our present crisis and had come to a conclusion. He said, "I have given this matter much thought, and I have only one thing to say; so listen carefully, for you will have to live with the decision you make. Once we terminate this conversation we shall never speak of it again." By this time my stomach was in knots, and I knew somehow that this decision was going to hurt. Then, in the very brief statement he made next, my world came crashing down all around me, leaving me drained and speechless. He continued: "I have decided that you can give up all these foolish ideas about college and have the love and protection of your family, or you can go ahead with your foolish plans to enter college. But the minute you walk out our door, consider it closed to you forever."

I was numb. I couldn't believe what I was hearing. It was unbelievable to me that my father would go to such extremes in order to prevent my leaving home. The feeling I had inside was one of complete despair, and he left me crying as I had never cried before.

After Dad had left, Mom came in to comfort me. She placed her hands on my shoulders and said, "Elizabeth,

I know this is a difficult decision you have to make, but I want you to think about this: Don't let emotion and 'old country' traditions hinder your future. You *are* and *always will be* my daughter. Your father can never take that away from me. I want you to go and take advantage of this wonderful opportunity. Make us all proud. Your father is slow to change, but give him time and pray for him. Please go with my blessing."

With great reluctance I left home that last Monday of August 1966. It was the most difficult decision I had ever had to make, for I knew full well the consequences of being disowned. That day was a turning point in my life in that my family ties and relationships could never be the same again—I had lost my father forever. I was frightened and lonely as I boarded the bus for college, and my heart was heavy for Mom and the family. I knew that life would never be as it had so long been. Mine was a tearful and sad departure. I cried most of the way to Texas, thinking about the family which I had lost.

All kinds of questions were going through my mind. The most persistent one was *Did I make the right decision?* At the time I had decided to go through with my decision to leave home, I was sure that my choice was the right one. But the stark reality of leaving my family behind, of being disowned from my relationship with them, had not, at that point, really begun to make its impact felt. I was alone and frightened, and the bus trip to southern Texas was bringing the reality of my being disowned into sharp focus.

I had much to overcome, for it was the first time I had ever been away from home. I was completely unaware of what to anticipate from the outside world and away from my protective family. The thought was frightening, and I knew that it would be a long time before I could ever feel safe and secure again. I could see in the eyes of the people around me on the bus that my fear and naïveté were obvious, and I felt helpless in my inability to conceal my feelings.

The strangers whom I encountered on the bus were, of course, of many characters. Some tried to comfort me, seeking to help me in my time of need; and I appreciated their concern. With this initial christening into the outside world, many things entered my mind. My fears grew as I traveled southward, and that nagging question concerning my decision to leave home began to surface once again.

Though I tried to be brave and to assure myself that things would be all right once I had arrived at my destination, I could not help but wonder if, in the final outcome, college would be worth the agony of my sacrifices. I had the comforting thought that my relatives would be waiting for me when I arrived in Texas, but I had a deeper feeling that kept warning me not to depend too much on this hope. And I prayed for strength to accept and deal with my future destiny.

When I arrived in Texas and no one was there to meet me at the station, I knew that one of my fears was already becoming a reality. I decided to call my aunt just in case she had not been sure of my arrival time. During our phone conversation, my aunt informed me that all of my relatives knew that I had been disowned by my family and consequently felt obligated to abide by my father's wishes. This meant, of course, that they would be unable to help me. While she felt sorry for me, she thought it best not to get involved with my family problem. She ended the conversation by wishing me the best. Under the circumstances, I was glad to have ended the conversation on this positive note. Feeling completely alone and lost, I hung up the phone.

Never in my life had I been so completely alone. In the cold and lonely atmosphere of the bus station, I tried to decide what to do next. The more I sat there, the more tempted I was to get on the next bus home and beg my father's forgiveness; but my pride would not let me do it. I reckoned with myself that I was going to have to make it alone, now or never.

I decided to go to the college and present my problems there. After placing my belongings in a locker at the bus station, I asked the ticket agent behind the counter how to get to the college. He gave me the directions; and since I was only about five blocks away, I decided to walk. Everyone I passed on the street seemed to be staring at me. I felt closed off from the new world around me, afraid and unsure of what I would find at the school when I arrived.

As I approached the campus, I saw lovers sitting under the big palm trees that surrounded the campus, looking as if they were oblivious to the hustle and bustle of other students and professors preparing for a new year at school. It was a hot and muggy day; and after the five-block walk from the bus station, I felt wet and sticky. I walked toward the largest building on campus, hoping that I could find help from someone inside. As I entered the front door, I felt the cool blast of air conditioning on my tired, hot body. The trip down to Texas had been long and tiring, and the weather was hot and humid. These conditions, combined with lack of rest, caused me to feel somewhat faint.

I inquired at the reception desk, asking where I might find someone to whom I could talk concerning personal problems. The woman at the desk pointed me in the direction of the dean's office, where she felt I could find help. I walked down to the office and told the secretary that I was enrolled for the fall term; but due to some personal problems, some of my plans had to be changed. She was very polite but cool, looking as if she had heard similar stories from many other students. Following a brief wait, I was ushered in to see the dean.

He was a man of average height, slightly overweight, bald, and wore glasses. He was wearing a short-sleeved shirt unbuttoned at the neck, with a loosened tie drooping over his protruding stomach. He looked as if he had been through a long, hard day, and I felt slightly guilty about burdening this man with some more problems. I found him to be very warm and understanding. The expression on his face as I told him my story showed a loving concern that I had witnessed many times before in past relationships with teachers.

He arranged for me to stay in the dormitory and to work for my room and board, finding me a job in the language department for $1.25 an hour. It wasn't much, but it was a beginning. I left his office feeling confident about my decision to stay at college, regardless of the unpleasant consequences I faced in my personal life for doing so. After picking up my luggage at the bus depot, I moved into my new home, room 233 in Emmett Hall Dormitory.

My two college years were a learning as well as a frustrating experience. I was a country bumpkin, without even much farm experience, and my naïveté was obvious. In the beginning I was depressed and extremely homesick, and the drab gray color of my dormitory room did not help my spirits. The room looked bare and lifeless with the lone bed, desk, and lamp, but I could not get in the mood to fix it up and make it more lively. My room in fact reflected my personality during my college years in Texas. Most of my depression had stemmed from the crisis which I had experienced at home. I wrote to Mother frequently, but never once received an answer. Later I learned that my father had forbidden her to write me, under the threat of physical abuse. If I had known the circumstances, I would not have put Mother through such a strain.

Most of my time in school was spent in one of four places: the library, where I studied; the language department, where I worked; the cafeteria, where I ate; and my dormitory room, where I slept. This was my world, and the occasions when I ventured out of this self-imposed restrictive environment were rare.

The frustrations of wanting to learn and be a good student, but of feeling burdened by the conditions I left at home, caused me to contemplate suicide. Alone in my room at night, I envisioned different ways to take my own life, thinking that if I did kill myself I could get even with my father. This was my prime motivation for thinking about killing myself—to get even. But after a while, when I would regain my senses, I would always reject the suicide idea, feeling that God did have a purpose for my life if I could just get through school and find it. It was a very trying and searching time for me; and I felt alone, deserted by God and my family.

I was finding the pressures of the outside world greater than I had expected them to be. I had left home after the start of the Vietnam War; and campus unrest, drugs, and hippie communes were all a part of my college experience. Confusion, along with unfamiliarity with campus life, was my constant companion. I was approached by all kinds of campus organizations, but I refused membership in them out of fear of being unacceptable to my peers. I kept pretty much to myself, as I had done in high school, and had only limited friendships. Though I became acquainted with many young adults from all walks of life and backgrounds, somehow I was always more attracted to students with serious problems, for many of whom I provided an ear. These times of counseling were also helpful for me in that they provided me with an excuse to put my own problems aside temporarily.

On the lighter side of my college life, in 1967 I ate my first hamburgers and french fries. This experience occurred when I was invited to dinner by a fellow student—my first date! I had a difficult time trying to decide whether to go on this first date; and Thomas, the young man who asked me out, seemed surprised at my innocence. He was not a very good-looking boy, but he had a kind heart. He quickly reckoned with my dilemma and proceeded to put me at ease with his witty and lighthearted nature. Before long we were both laughing and joking as we walked the three short blocks to the restaurant. Once again I had been fortunate to have made such a nice acquaintance at such an important time in my life.

After dinner, Thomas walked with me back to the dormitory, where we said goodnight. In a quick move that took me by surprise, he leaned down and gently kissed me on the cheek. I was stunned for a moment, but soon regained my composure and thanked him for the nice evening by shaking his hand. It was an awkward time, but I managed to stumble through the formalities of saying goodnight. Although he never asked me out again, we remained friends as long as we attended the same college. After this introduction into the world of boy-girl relationships, I was never again hesitant to accept a date from a nice-looking, well-mannered boy.

During my college years in Texas, I was also faced with the temptation to use drugs. Practically everyone I knew at college was taking drugs or knew where to get them. Many students with problems were vulnerable and succumbed to the cheap thrills being offered by those who sold drugs. I remember seeing many students suffer under the influence of drugs as they tried in vain to forget their problems by taking heroin, sniffing cocaine, smoking marijuana, or getting drunk on alcohol. The temptation to join the crowd and take something to erase my problems, if even for a short while, was great; but I knew that once the power of the drug wore off, the problems would still be there. Though I was vulnerable, I was not weak enough to deny my responsibility and take the easy way out. There were numerous times when I was so low that nothing in life seemed to matter. Only with God's help was I able to survive those times of temptation and to reject the lower paths I could have followed.

Finally, after two years of agony and unhappiness, Dr. Cooper, one of my professors, called me into his office. Dr. Cooper was one of the few Anglo professors at this predominantly Mexican-American school. He was a large man, standing well over six feet tall, with the physique of a man who kept himself in top physical condition. His hair was dark brown, matching the color of his eyes. I was particularly drawn to Dr. Cooper and felt at ease when we spoke, but today he seemed worried.

He began our conversation with small talk about the weather and played with the items atop his desk in a fidgety manner. After about ten minutes he said abruptly, "Let's talk about your life, beginning with your life as a migrant, and your relationship to your family." We discussed my life from its start to the present for some two hours, then finally came to my future. My future was something I hadn't thought about since I had arrived on campus. Somehow my future had lost its importance during those two years. I really had no one with whom to share my dreams; besides, by that time, I wasn't dreaming much anyway.

Dr. Cooper informed me that I had no future unless I really wanted to have it. He said those magic words, "It's time for you to go home and make everything right with yourself and your family." I wanted desperately to go home, but I told him that I had been disowned and that this meant I was forbidden ever to go home again. He said, "This is 1968! No one gets disowned anymore. This is the twentieth century; old traditions are gone forever!" Then he hit a nerve—he said, "It is time to swallow your pride and be realistic. You are not functioning as a human. You are walking around like a zombie. Your mind is at home. Go home! That is the only way you are going to find peace of mind, and perhaps your future will be saved."

By the next day I was packed and ready to go. Dr. Cooper bought me a bus ticket home and drove me to the bus station. I am forever in debt to him for encouraging me to make the decision to return home. Finally, I was really on my way home! Just the thought was sweet and made me peaceful. I knew that I would not be well received by my father and brothers, but I was more than willing to face the consequences just to know and see for myself that those whom I loved were all right. The thought of going home was so wonderful that nothing could mar my joy and great expectation.

I had written to my mother earlier, informing her of my decision to come home and face the consequences. I prayed for the strength to survive the ordeal and a chance to make peace with the family I had left two years earlier. On the long bus ride home, I prepared myself for an unwelcome reception.

As the bus entered my hometown, many pleasant and not-so-pleasant memories entered my mind. Though I was beginning to feel like the prodigal returning home, somehow I could not feel guilty over what I had done. Those two years in Texas, however miserable they may have been, were growing years; and I knew that I would never again be able to live with my family.

As we neared the bus station, my heart was beating frantically as my eyes scanned the crowd of people in the depot. I was desperate as the bus came to a halt; there was still no sign of my mother. I disembarked and slowly made my way over to where the luggage was being unloaded. As I waited for the familiar sight of my worn, brown suitcase, I felt a hand upon my shoulder. I quickly spun around and was greeted with the warm, loving smile and bright black eyes of my mother. It was the best therapy for my heart and soul just to see her and to hold her close. Following an exchange of hugs we began the short walk from the bus depot to our home.

When we arrived, my father would have nothing to do with me. He made it clear that I could stay only until I could find another place to live. I was prepared for this reaction and realized that my visit at home would be brief. After staying for two months and satisfying my mind on the condition of my parents and brothers, seeing for myself that all was as well as could be expected, I was ready to move on and to try to salvage my future. This time I knew that I could make it because I could be keeping close contact with Mother. Never again would I be alone.

4
A Sign of Hope

I am living proof that radical change is a possibility, something that can and does occur. This is no longer a speculation but is a fact of experience. During the first fourteen years of my life, I was living out my simple and uncomplicated existence from the back of our truck home. Life was eminently predictable for me and my family, for we merely repeated our migrant cycle, never realizing how small and limited our world was. There was, for us, no Rufus Jones or Thomas Kelly to give us any remote insight to our poverty-stricken spiritual life. In fact, religion had negative overtones for us because of our unfortunate experiences with and our ignorance of the subject.

My first memory of a religious encounter concerns an experience I had when I was about six years old. In our truck home Mother had hung a picture of Christ, before which she always lit a candle. This candlelighting ceremony did not reflect a rational decision, but the Roman Catholic influence with which she had always been surrounded. I am sure, however, that this practice was of a serious nature and an expression of genuine devotion. For us children, however, it was meaningless or even comical. We made finger puppets on the wall by the light reflected from the candle. Because my mother felt that practicing her religion was a serious duty, we were punished for our childish pranks.

In spite of our obvious spiritual poverty, I can see now that my mother did something valuable in that she provided me with a sense of good behavior. She taught me the finer traditions of our culture—the arts of sewing, fine crocheting, Spanish cooking, and other refined talents that she possessed. She was never in any sense permissive, and she never for a moment allowed me to use vulgar language or to dress in slacks, shorts, or revealing clothes of any kind. All alcohol and tobacco were strictly excluded from our lives. Despite Mother's insistence on high standards for her children, however, my father finally became an alcoholic. This development made me realize that it was my mother who had set the standards for my life. Though my mother was and still is in many ways ignorant, I owe her a great deal, for she always encouraged me to go forward. In the words of Thomas Carlyle concerning his humble father, she launched me into a world that she had never been permitted to visit.

Due to their lack of religious training, my parents, along with other migrant families, were highly superstitious. For example, they believed in the "evil eye." When I was about nine years old I came down with influenza and was sick for several days. Dad, deeply worried, took me out into the woods to an anthill filled with big red ants. He made me jump over the anthill in the form of a cross, while he recited some prayer and ended it with "in the name of the Father, the Son, and the Holy Ghost."

For me the ceremony was a great mystery; all I understood was that I received many ant bites. For my father it was an attempt to drive away the evil spirits that were making me sick. I do not know whether it was the ant bites or my father's ritual that was successful; but in any case, I did get well. However, from that time on I kept my fingers crossed, hoping that I would not get sick again and have to share in a ridiculous ritual.

The first important change in my impoverished spiritual life came about because of a small Baptist mission, which was our chief sign of hope after we became settled migrants. The Southern Baptist Mission Church stood as a spiritual fortress for me and my mother during my most difficult days at home. Within the walls of this shaky wooden structure, I found a retreat from the world of violence, poverty, and deprivation that characterized the Mexican subculture. The church building is considered an eyesore in the community today; but when I was growing up it was a beautiful, well-kept structure, radiating faith from within and offering hope to all who entered. It became a symbol of reassurance for me and for all others who sought a better life and a deeper understanding of spiritual realities.

Immediately after settling in our new community, we

were visited by two missionaries from Argentina who had started the mission church just two years before. Both were young and exhibited a strong sense of enthusiasm for their calling. Pablo was short and trim, with hazel eyes and thinning brown hair. His smile was a vivid contrast to the drab surroundings in our living room. Pedro was tall and slender, possessing blondish hair and dark blue eyes. He seemed more reserved than Pablo; but when he did speak, his voice was strong and resonant. He was an effective speaker.

I was soon impressed both by their sensitivity and their strong Christian faith. They wanted to help us, not just because helping people was their job or because they saw us as miserable sinners who were to be conquered for the cause of Christ. Their understanding of mission was much deeper, combining concern for both our physical and our spiritual well-being. These two workers for Christ recognized us as human beings in our own right and as sons and daughters of God who were in need of their ministry. Their attitude was one of patience, understanding, and, most of all, a pervading sense of love for their fellow men and women. During this first encounter Mother and I promised to attend worship the following week. In the meantime they invited us to visit their mission store, which carried a good supply of used clothing, household items, and toys. We thanked them for their concern. Following a time of prayer together, they gave me a Bible and quietly left.

Mother felt good about our encounter with the two

missionaries. Because the visit meant a great deal to her, she wasted no time in making plans and preparations for Sunday. I was a bit more hesitant, for I had never been exposed to any religion other than folk Catholicism. I wasn't sure that attending this mission was the right thing to do. I thought about this prospect a great deal during the week and became even more intrigued as I, for the first time, began to read the Bible that the missionaries had left me. Reading in Genesis about God's creation was a new experience, and my imagination drew a vivid picture of the Garden of Eden. There was much that I did not understand; and some of my uneasiness about the approaching Sunday turned into anxious anticipation, for I wanted to hear what the missionaries had to say about the things I was reading.

Since my mother could not read well, even in Spanish, I would relate to her what I was learning. By the time Sunday arrived, we were both ready to share what we were learning and to ask questions about things we did not understand. I don't know about Mom, but I had butterflies in my stomach that Sunday morning as we left our home for the short, five-block walk to the mission church. As we went through the large wooden doors we were greeted by the smiling face of Pablo. He ushered us into the sanctuary, where we were greeted by many of our migrant friends. Seeing so many people we knew helped us to relax, and the splendor of the stained-glass windows filled me with wonder.

As we sat down on one of the hardwood pews, I

noticed a picture of Christ at the front of the room. He was kneeling in prayer beside a rock, looking upward into the heavens. It was a beautiful sight; and in years to come this picture was destined to serve me as a model of strength, around which my life would evolve. I also noticed, on the wall next to me, a plaque that recorded the history of the mission building. I was amazed to learn that the building had once belonged to the Roman Catholic Church. This knowledge helped to ease my anxiety about attending a non-Catholic worship service.

I don't know what it was that kept nagging me about going to a Protestant church. Perhaps it was Dad's fierce negative attitude about what Mother and I were doing. He felt that we were somehow deserting him and his faith, even though he could barely be labeled a nominal Catholic. In my mind there was a sharp contrast between his angered face and the peaceful outer surroundings. Before the worship service began my feelings were in turmoil.

All fears and doubts were swept away, however, as Mother and I listened to a message based upon the Sermon on the Mount. During the message I glanced over at Mom, who smiled softly back at me. We were both lifted spiritually by the words of Pedro. Mother and I had decided together, though the expression was nonverbal, that we had actually found a spiritual home.

Once again new doors were opened for me. It did not take long for us to involve ourselves totally with the church. Mother became the treasurer of the church, and

I soon became the fifth- and sixth-grade teacher in the Sunday School. I studied the Bible intensely in preparation for each Sunday School lesson I was to teach, for the task was not something to be taken lightly. I truly believed that the moral and spiritual development of those fifth- and sixth-grade children was in my hands. Having experienced a home situation similar to that of most of them, the awesome responsibility of what I had been charged to do became almost overwhelming.

Many of my experiences in that Sunday-morning class come readily to mind today, but one incident stands out above the rest. One Palm Sunday I was reading to the children the events of Jesus' last week on earth. I had read the fifteenth chapter of Mark many times, but never was I moved quite so deeply as when I read this chapter to those children on that balmy spring day in 1964. My class was perfectly silent as I read the part where Pilate asked Jesus, "Art thou the King of the Jews?" The picture of the strong, silent Christ standing before the Roman governor was a gripping scene in my mind's eye. Later in the chapter I read about how the crowd cried, "Crucify him!" and had to explain the meaning of *crucify* to a group of children who were not shocked by the use of violence.

But as I read about how the crowd mocked him and spit on him, I was moved to tears. My small, quiet band of little Mexican Christians did not understand this outburst of emotion. Though I quickly composed myself, before I could continue to read, Angela, one of my pupils, sought to comfort me. In a trembling, weak voice she said, "Don't cry, Miss Loza, it's almost Easter!" In her innocent way, Angela had moved my thoughts from the crucifixion to the resurrection. I am still amazed that God chose a little girl to share a profound truth with me.

Week after week I continued to find spiritual help in the mission church. While the Sunday-morning worship services were always uplifting, the activities during the week were just as important to my spiritual development. The building was in constant use, for a stream of migrants and other low-income families went in and out of the church basement, where the mission store was located. This store provided blankets, clothing, and canned goods at reduced prices for those in need. The Wednesday-night prayer meeting not only helped my religious life, but gave me an excuse to get out of my strictly run home. There were sewing classes that met at the mission after school, as well as self-help programs designed to help Mexican-Americans adjust to their new environment. These classes helped in the areas of money management, reading, and personal hygiene.

I soon discovered that the mission was much more than just a place of worship. Although the worship life of the church was central, the missionaries recognized that worship did little good if it was not combined with a sincere desire to help change daily life. The Mexican-American subculture within my home community needed something more than just spiritual nourishment, for the people were steeped in poverty and lacked many physical necessities.

So, while our inner lives were being given spiritual food, our outer lives were being helped through the mission store, special classes, and the personal ministry of Pablo and Pedro. This ministry to the whole person greatly affected me in my youth, and I still consider this approach to missions the only valid way to carry the banner of Christ among the homeless, deprived people in the world today.

One of the greatest helps the mission provided me with was in the area of prayer. I had prayed many times before I became a member of the mission, but I did not truly understand its deeper meaning until I shared in a prayer group led by Pedro. Before this prayer-group experience, I had always used prayer as a vehicle to get special favors from God. It was my "secret weapon" to get what I wanted. I used prayer constantly, asking for everything from revenge on a fellow schoolmate to a new pair of shoes. I had been indiscriminate in my use of prayer, feeling secure in the knowledge that God would never let me down. This childish understanding of prayer was severely shaken when I did not receive the asked-for pair of shoes or did not witness any tragedy in the life of the schoolmate for whom I sought revenge. I mentioned this frustration in my prayer group and soon gained new insight into the use and meaning of prayer. Without making me feel ignorant for raising this issue, Pedro told me and the group what he considered to be the purpose of prayer.

He said, "Elizabeth, it is important for you to learn how to listen to God, not just beg of him. I believe the purpose of prayer is not to tell God what you want, but to find out from God what he wants of you." This was a new insight for me, and the gentle way in which Pedro expressed himself told me that he knew what he was talking about.

After prayer meeting had adjourned, I stayed to talk further with Pedro and sought his counsel concerning this new approach to prayer. On this occasion he told me how God was working in his life, giving him strength to minister in a new land to an almost forgotten people. His story about how he came to Christ and decided to give his life to his service and to the betterment of humankind touched me deeply. He had given up a fine home and job security in his native land so that he could enter the ministry. His eyes filled with tears, and it was as though he was back in Argentina as he told me about his homeland and family.

"I had a wonderful life in my homeland," he said, "but God needed me here, so I came."

"But how did God tell you he wanted you here?" I asked in my inquisitive way.

"Elizabeth," he began the slow deliberate reply, "the Lord speaks to all of us in our varying conditions and circumstances. Sometimes we choose to listen, and sometimes we refuse his gentle nudging, feeling that we can best handle our affairs alone. Jesus Christ has entered into my life in such a way that I know how, where, and when he wants to use my life for his purposes. When word reached me about the need for a missionary among the Mexican migrant people in this area, I knew immediately that this was the work for which God had been preparing me. Sometimes it is more difficult to discern what the Lord would have me do, and only after long periods of prayer and frustration do I finally realize what God would have me do in a particular situation. My advice to you is to remain open in your life of prayer; and when God has a particular ministry for you to do, somehow you will know what it is."

I left the mission that evening almost in a trance, for I was trying to sort out in my mind all that I had heard. I do not remember my walk home, but I shall never forget the beautiful testimony of Pedro as he related his witness of the experience of God in his life. I wanted the same joy, and that night I prayed long and hard for God to use me for his purposes as he had used Pedro. It is difficult to explain in written words what happened next, except to say that I knew beyond a doubt that God was in my room with me, encircling me with his love, as if to say, "Lo, I am with you always, even unto the end of the world."

After four years of meaningful ministry, Pablo and Pedro felt free to return to their native land. I had mixed feelings about their leaving, and I am sure the other members felt the same. We had developed a dependence on these men that was not healthy, but the thought of their leaving made us fear for the survival of our mission. This, we discovered later, was a silly thought, for not only were we strong enough to continue; we also secured the leadership of Mary and Wayne Smith, who brought a new dimension to our lives.

Wayne and Mary Smith were called from a nearby Southern Baptist church to serve our mission. Since they came just a year before I left for college, their ministry made a deep and lasting impression upon me, helping to carry me through my most difficult years away from home. They did much to educate me in understanding and accepting myself as well as the ways of Americans. They encouraged me to use my talents and helped me express my deep feelings and fears. Most of all, they were able to give me the confidence I needed to reach goals that were seemingly impossible for a little migrant girl. Through persistence they were able to build up my self-esteem and to make the obstacles in my life turn into challenges to be conquered instead of reasons for defeat. They implanted in me the seed of deep Christian commitment and faith, which blossomed when I needed it most. There are not enough words to describe or express the wonderful ministry of this Christian team. Their work can only be evaluated in terms of the life changes among my people.

Under the leadership of Mary and Wayne, many more programs for the Mexican migrant community were established. These programs were a result of their Christian commitment to the betterment of humankind and their knowledge about administration, which Pedro and Pablo did not possess. Also, because Mary and Wayne were Anglo, they were able to mingle freely in the white community. Pedro and Pablo had been outcasts. This helped to win support from the business community, whose donations were always welcome.

A good example of the new ministry came when the Smiths were able to obtain sponsors for those of us who could read and write English and Spanish, so that we could go to the University of Kansas and learn the Frank Laubach teaching method, "Each One Teach One." They hoped that we could learn this method of teaching so that we might help our fellow migrants. Most of the members of the mission could not read or write well in either Spanish or English, but their hunger to learn and understand the Scriptures was tremendous. There were six of us who made the four-hundred-mile trip to Lawrence, which included a great time of fellowship together as well as the opportunity to gain valuable knowledge for our reading and writing ministry.

Mary set up an evening class for mission members and began the slow, agonizing process of teaching us the Laubach method. Before long, however, as results could be seen, we opened the class to others in the community. The response was overwhelming; and while we were helping the illiterate to read and write, we were able at the same time to make a powerful witness for Jesus Christ. This ability resulted in a growth in membership and a boost in morale for our leaders.

The course on reading and writing was an important first step in the ministry of the Smiths, but many other services followed. One service that was of great help to us was family counseling. This program dealt mostly with personal family problems, particularly those connected with alcoholism—which is a major social problem in the Mexican migrant subculture and invariably leads to family tension and suffering. There were many, my family included, who suffered when the husband would take his earnings and spend them on alcohol. The wife and children would find themselves in need of food and other essential supplies.

The situation was made worse when the wife joined the husband in getting drunk, thus leaving the children in need of care. The doors of the Baptist mission were always open to help with such problems. The family counseling service provided understanding comfort to those in need, encouragement to continue, and food to hold them over until the next paycheck arrived. Besides helping when crises occurred, Wayne Smith would seek out the husband or wife and try to help him or her deal with the problem of dependence on alcohol. This Christian approach to the problem made the program a success, and many families were saved from ruin because of it.

My mother is still an active member of this mission, and her enthusiasm has not changed in the fourteen years during which she has been a member. In these changing times government programs and ecumenical groups have taken over many of the programs begun by the Baptist mission, but these are supported and many times controlled by its members. In this wider context the mission's love and concern for humankind continues in abundance. Their membership remains small—they are a minority within a minority—but it continues to be active in spirit. Mother now assures me that the Christian work begun with Pedro and Pablo and continued with the Smiths is still reaching lives that would otherwise have no contact with the Christian faith. I know that she is telling me the truth, for she is a radiant example of the spiritual nurture that took place within the walls of that little Baptist mission.

My religious development in the mission prepared me for weathering one of the most challenging and questioning phases of my life. Being alone in college without a family was difficult, but being alone and a professed Christian was even more so. I am sure that life would not have been so hard had I attended a Christian school, but the lack of money made that impossible.

I have already mentioned that my college years were those at the height of the drug movement, the Vietnam war, and the hippie communes. Many students were taking drugs and were active in political causes I did not understand. The pressures of these elements were difficult to bear for a naive and ignorant student. Afraid of controversy concerning causes I did not fully comprehend, I spent many lonely hours in my own little world, often daydreaming of my past and ignoring the present. It was too difficult to face. I found many moments of comfort when I recalled happier times in the mission and in the security of my family. Memories of loving faces of the mission members crowded my troubled mind, making me extremely homesick. Some of the members, realizing my sad fate, wrote me and gave me encouragement. They assured me of their prayers, and their welcome letters always boosted my battered spirit.

Even so, the sad state of my life was in need of some strong spiritual uplift. My religious life had reached a stage of confusion; "God is Dead" was a common saying around campus. Students were living together in communes, where they experimented with drugs. Some believed that God could be reached through LSD and in an imaginary simple world in their style of living.

All of these experiences were heavy on my heart when I finally returned home. Because I had greatly missed my mission church while at school, I looked forward to seeing the Smiths and worshiping as I had done before I went away. Leaving the house to go to church was an emotional experience. Mother had gone to Sunday School, so I left alone. As I approached the little mission, I had the same feeling that I had experienced the very first time I had attended. I stopped and stared from a distance as I watched people arriving. After waiting until I was sure that all who were coming to worship had entered the sanctuary, I approached the door. Soon I could hear singing, and the sweet melody of the hymn "In the Garden" beckoned me to enter.

With tears in my eyes I climbed the stairs, which led into what was for me a most sacred place.

I slowly opened the door and was quickly swept into an atmosphere of worship. I quietly walked to the third row from the front and took a seat next to my mother. She smiled and shared her hymnal with me for the last stanza of the hymn. As we were singing, my mind wandered to the time when God had touched me with his love for the first time in this sanctuary; and I remembered how I had survived the storm of being disowned, going to college, and taking the step to return home. The immediate past was difficult to face, but the future was even more ominous. As I listened to Wayne read the Scriptures, I felt a sense of reassurance come over me—the same feeling I had experienced so many times in my life—and I felt certain of God's leading.

The Southern Baptist mission had begun a process that had forced me to study life and to question what my future life would be. I refused to accept the notion that, since I was born a migrant, I was to remain in the traditional migrant pattern throughout my earthly life. But if my life was going to change, how would that change take place? In what direction would I go? With these questions burning in my mind, I made frequent visits to the little mission chapel during those brief weeks at home upon my return from college. Believing in the power of prayer, I sat for long periods of time, openly talking to God and receiving in return a sureness of mind and a new assurance about life.

During my periods of solitude, while sitting in perfect

stillness, I felt the fears and tensions of my outward life drain away. My times of prayer and meditation awakened within me a new awareness of my calling. *How often,* I thought, *our essential purpose in this life is hidden in our outward activities and lost in the day-to-day struggles for existence.* But in quiet times with God, such as my times of worship in the little chapel of the mission church, the inner self is awakened; and our true calling is lifted out of the mire of life's confusion and set before us in a new and exciting way.

This is what happened to me. I know from experience that life is unequal. It is true that some days are greater than some years. I can remember dark periods in my life when all seemed hopeless. The drudgery of routine daily living could keep me occupied for long periods of time with little relief. And then, like a beam of light across a black sky, a new insight would capture my mind and spirit. Suddenly I was involved in a totally new way of thinking.

Such a beam of light entered my life during my transition time from college in Texas to business school in Wichita. I was awakened during this critical juncture to a new understanding of my purpose. I began to consider seriously the Christian ministry as my life's vocation. Suddenly, all that had gone before—all of my suffering, all of the hard work, all of the inner struggling that had left me depressed and lonely—began to make sense. I knew that all that was to come in my new environment would revolve around this central calling to minister. The void in my life was being filled to overflowing by

Jesus Christ; and, although my outer life was still a mass of confusion, my inner life was beginning to point in a purposeful direction. My little home mission had planted within me a seed of hope, which Christ was bringing to blossom in a new purpose for my life. For the planting of this seed and for the loving expressions of concern for me as a person, I am eternally grateful.

5
The Conjunct Life

My life was changing drastically. I knew that I ought to serve in some area of the Christian ministry, but I also needed to earn some sort of living. I resolved to delay my liberal arts education in favor of learning some business skills so I could earn some money. This decision prompted me to seek a place where I could obtain quick employment and also a place to live. Therefore, in the autumn of 1968 I settled in Wichita, where I enrolled in a business school and also found a good job in a local hospital.

The mental depression that I had experienced was leaving me, and I was soon doing well in both enterprises. The year went by quickly, and I completed my studies at the business school. Not feeling satisfied, however, as far as educational achievements were concerned, I enrolled in Wichita State University and expected to concentrate in the areas of Spanish and sociology.

It was 1968, and the Peace Movement was in full

swing. During this time I met my future husband and learned about the Religious Society of Friends (Quakers). Though I was, by infant baptism, a Roman Catholic, I had become a Southern Baptist in the little mission church in our settled community. Upon my arrival in Wichita, I roomed with another Southern Baptist girl. She gave me the encouragement to learn more about what was called the Peace Movement. I had read in the newspaper that Friends University was going to have a peace vigil, protesting the Vietnam war. When I discussed this with my roommate, however, she explained to me that the announced event was Communist inspired and that the only attenders would be Communists. Consequently, she advised me not to go. But I was stubborn and curious (I had never seen a Communist), and I made up my mind to participate.

When I arrived at the campus of Friends University, all I saw was a group of students and adults with their heads bowed in silent prayer. This affected me deeply, for I had not anticipated any such sight. Since I was looking for a group of Communists, I was truly shocked. Leading the group in prayer was a handsome young man whom I met shortly after the vigil ended. It turned out that he was a Quaker, a member of a religion I thought was dead, and that he was the son of a Quaker minister. This was strange to me because the one thing I thought I knew about Quakers was that they had no ministers. (I learned later about the evolution of the pastoral system among Friends and could then begin to tie things together.) For me it was a delightful encounter, and a truly momentous one.

James Newby and I began dating in October 1968. We were first attracted through our mutual interests concerning man's inhumanity to man. But, as time went by, we discovered that our interest in social problems was becoming secondary to our interest in each other. As love was beginning to develop between us, I was unsure just how to handle my feelings. This was the first time I had ever experienced the joy that can come from a love relationship, and I was a bit frightened when my logical self was quickly overcome by my emotional feelings.

Acting in ways in which I had never acted before, I felt free to share with James both my problems and my concerns. I was becoming liberated from family ties that had kept me feeling guilty because I had left home. James and I talked for hours about the many exciting possibilities that life had to offer—all we had to do was place our faith in God and take advantage of the opportunities that were being made available for spiritual and intellectual growth. I looked forward to every day; and, following a ten-month courtship, we became engaged in July 1969.

My mother, whom I had kept informed on every aspect of our courtship, was thrilled and excited about the way in which our relationship had developed. She adored James and his family from the beginning. Dad, however, had not been informed; and when he was finally told, he was upset. In his eyes I was once again rebelling against him by marrying out of my race and religion. By this time, however, I had grown to understand my father's love of tradition. And after being with James for ten months, I had gained enough courage not to let my father's tirades bother me. I know now that even though my father has shown it in a peculiar way, he always has had a deep love for me.

I informed James that he must ask my parents for my hand in marriage, as this particular step involves great significance for the entire family. I felt that as long as I was trying to rebuild bridges, there was no point in avoiding any of the necessary steps. Besides, I felt very strongly about doing things traditionally in order to try to reach my father. Because this effort was not too much to ask of me, I was ready to compromise.

James responded calmly, "I'll take care of everything; don't worry about it." *Ha*, I thought, *you don't know my family!* My future husband was almost too relaxed, and his calmness concerned me; but since I had complete confidence in him, I tried not to worry.

As it turned out, James sent his parents to ask for my hand in marriage. No wonder he was calm, cool, and collected! Upon their arrival my mother welcomed them, but my father was nowhere to be found. My mother, however, felt that since Dad was not there, she should take the responsibility upon herself to give them permission for James and me to marry. Since this was stepping out of a mother's role, I must say she was very brave to have done what she did.

My brother's wife informed me that Dad came storming in after the Newbys had left, demanding to know what they wanted. My mother told him that he was well aware of why they had come and that, since he could not be found, she had taken the responsibility of giving permission for me to marry into a family gracious enough to do the right thing by seeking their blessing. But she didn't stop there! She also informed my father that he was to be at University Friends Church in Wichita on December 21 to give me away and that if he was not there, he'd better not be at home when she got back from the wedding!

This was shocking for my father to hear, since my mother had never before defied him. As he was the head of our family, his word had always been the law. I must say that I was glad to hear about my mother's courage, and I wished that she had shown it more often. She has been too quiet in accepting her passive role, while my father has been stubborn and wrong.

The end result of all this was that my father did actually arrive to give me away, but just five minutes before the wedding ceremony was to begin. Because he had not been at the rehearsal, he didn't know what he was supposed to do. So as we walked down the aisle, I explained to him in Spanish what he was to say. Because he stepped on my train all the way, it took at least five to seven minutes for us to reach the front of the meetinghouse. Once we were at the front, he stood on my train so that I could not even move.

My father-in-law, who was conducting our wedding, noticed my dilemma and proceeded with the ceremony.

When he asked, "Who gives the bride away?" my father, instead of saying "Her mother and I," answered, "Herself and her mother." Luckily, since he spoke in Spanish, the others did not know what he had said. The ceremony ended without further embarrassing incidents, and James and I were really married.

After the hectic events involved with the wedding preparations, we were more than ready for our honeymoon. We spent a memorable week in Denver, trying to ski, but, more importantly, just enjoying each other's company. It ended all too soon. Since we were both employed, we had to return to our jobs immediately following our week in Denver. James was still a student at Friends University; and we decided, because of financial necessity, to postpone any further education for me.

Toward the end of his college career James decided to become a Quaker pastor. This came as a surprise to me, but not to his family. Three out of the last four generations of Newby men have entered the Quaker ministry. Having missed all the signs along the way that he was leaning in the direction of the pastoral ministry, I was caught unprepared. In retrospect, though, I can now see his development much more clearly; and our lives have been enriched by our association with the congregations that we have already served.

In two major ways my present life is radically different from the one in which I grew up. In the first place, I have a changed view of what a family can be, especially in the affection and mutual confidence that can be enjoyed by husband and wife. I am sorry for my mother because she has never known the kind of marital bliss that I now experience. In the second place, I have entered a large world in which there are no limits to the ideas I can entertain and the resources on which I can draw. I have found that I can learn not merely from the Mexican-American culture, but also from every culture. My chief means of doing so is the printed word. Since these two exciting differences in life-style have meant so much to me, I should like to try to describe what happened to a migrant girl when she was liberated from the cycle of poverty, ignorance, and the terrible home life in which she has been reared.

Sharing her life, her hopes, and her dreams with her mate is the most beautiful and enriching experience that can happen to any woman. To be able to express openly her pain and to find comfort, to be able to discuss her hopes and to find encouragement, to share love without fear of being rejected: these are integral to the life which I have found with James Newby. Because we share everything that occurs in our individual lives, our work has become a team experience.

I must admit that when I left home, marriage was the last thing I wanted. Throughout my life I had witnessed nothing but the worst aspects of married life, and I was not anxious to create a relationship that would stifle my intellectual and spiritual development as my mother's development had been stifled in her marriage. I did not intend to be locked into a relationship in which there was no mutual sharing of life's experiences or mutual trust and forgiveness between husband and wife. By accepting the fact that I could no longer live with my family, I was declaring my freedom from the bondage that does not allow a woman to attain her full God-given potential. At first, because I saw marriage as a part of that bondage, naturally I wanted nothing to do with it.

Something occurred eventually to produce a radical change in my thinking: I met James Newby. He has given me a new vision of the possibilities of marriage. He neither places me on a pedestal nor sees me as a mere producer of children. He loves me for myself, and I love him for himself. Consequently, I feel extremely lucky. We have discovered that two people can be perfectly yoked without a loss of identity on the part of either. James wants to be the best spiritual leader he can become, while I want to be the best writer I can become; we seek to help each other achieve our mutual purposes. The yoke philosophy has provided us with a model. According to this model, my husband is not the dominating male; nor is he henpecked. We have found a third way!

Through our daughter Alicia Marie our love has been greatly enriched. Alicia is a beautiful little girl, inheriting her mother's brown skin and her father's fat cheeks, big brown eyes, and long eyelashes. When Alicia was born in February 1972, James and I were unaware of what would be the effect of this event upon our married life. Though we looked forward to our child's birth with great expectations, underneath there was the feeling that we were unqualified to raise a child in the kind of world in which we then lived. Since her mother was of Latin descent and her father was Anglo, what would a mixed child have to face in a world of prejudice and discrimination?

The more James and I thought about this question, the more we came to realize that we asked not because we were trying to find a solution to the problem of race prejudice, but because the question was enabling us to deny our responsibility to our world and God. By simply raising this question, we were helping to perpetuate the problem instead of working toward a solution. The moment we began dwelling upon the positive aspects of child-rearing, we were able to prepare ourselves for the job that God had given us to do.

Raising a child is a difficult task. We live in a society and a world where there are many value choices for children to make, and they can certainly confuse unsuspecting persons. We cannot, however, throw up our arms in disgust and exclaim, "What's the use!" By doing this we neglect our responsibility to God and the world. The answer lies in raising each child in a setting where intelligible values and concerns will become guiding lights. Responsible Christianity means raising responsible Christian children who can make moral decisions that will help our world.

Alicia has been a joy in our lives, and we are both thrilled with her development. We *are* concerned with her future, and at times we fret about the world's condition; but we do not allow the "what is" in our world to overshadow the vision of "what could be."

The religious dimension of our family life is the basis of our life together. We have found that when we come together for prayer and Bible reading, our lives are magnified and unified. With our busy schedules, these times of worship are spiritual experiences to which James, Alicia, and I look forward and which we treasure. Although the idea of God is difficult for her to grasp, Alicia has learned to pray. Her favorite part is saying "Amen," which she exclaims so that all of our neighbors are aware that our time of worship has concluded!

Such regular family worship was never a part of my migrant life. It seemed that there was little to unite us spiritually as a family. Had it not been for my mother's insistence, I would never have had any exposure to Christianity in the home. My mother had many subtle ways of making her children know that, rude as it was, ours was meant to be a Christian home. She did so by references to Jesus Christ. But praying together as a family, finding spiritual resources for our living, was not part of our daily lives. Perhaps this is why these times of devotions with James and Alicia are so meaningful to me. All of us have grown spiritually as a result, and I am very thankful for the inner strength that our worship has provided.

We are living today in an age that makes tremendous demands upon the family unit. Each member of the family has his special activities: the son and daughter are occupied at an increasing rate by peer group and school activities; the husband and father has his club, golf date, bowling league, or continuing education classes that are required by his place of employment; the wife and mother is either busy working outside the home to supplement the family income, going to college, or rushing around reminding others of their next appointments. Where in this familiar situation is there to be any kind of spiritual growth and family unity?

It might be said that Sunday-morning worship produces family togetherness and spiritual nourishment. Corporate worship with fellow Christians is very important, and I do not intend here to belittle its value; but one or two hours a week is too little time to devote to something as important as the development of the spiritual life. We must somehow, in our busy schedules, make time for family prayer and devotions. The trite saying "The family that prays together stays together" holds more meaning than we might at first think. To engage with one's spouse and children in daily devotions and prayer is the most satisfying and spiritually enriching experience that can come to a person during the day. By taking this time to gather inner spiritual strength and to unite the family, I am taking what I believe to be the major step in assuring the survival of the family unit in an age when this unity is in a state of constant threat.

Though, under the influence of the mission, I studied the Bible and started to read more about the Christian life, I nevertheless began to have questions. Many times I could not get satisfactory answers from leaders of the local mission. In short, I was becoming confused about my religious beliefs. My first experience of college provided me with little help; and by the time I returned home, after much unhappiness and suffering, I was full of doubts. I had also acquired enough experience to know that religious leaders were sometimes personally untrustworthy. Some who called themselves servants of God were, I discovered, in reality self-seeking manipulators of other people. Because I had expected religious leaders to demonstrate uniformly high standards of character, this was a serious shock to me. Dissatisfied with the lack of intellectual inquiry concerning troublesome religious questions, I searched for a faith that could meet my inner spiritual needs, endure honest questioning, and serve the social needs of my fellowmen.

My greatest spiritual indebtedness, at this point, involved my father-in-law, Richard Newby, who had the courage to care. He introduced me to the writings of many great spiritual leaders, among them Thomas Kelly, Rufus Jones, and D. Elton Trueblood. Through the writings of these men I discovered Christ—not as a word of incantation and not merely as one who lived long ago, but as a Living Presence. It came as a great surprise to me that Christ can be my present teacher, here and now. In a Christ-centered faith I have found it possible to combine the needs of both mind and heart, of both service and devotion. In short, I was drawn to see that the choice between a personal gospel and a social gospel is unnecessary and that it is possible to be committed to Christ with full intellectual integrity.

In my Yokefellow Academy studies I have, by good fortune, been introduced to the vision of spiritual wholeness. Consequently, I now refuse to be stereotyped by any one label, theological or cultural. A great light dawned when I saw that I could be both rational and evangelical in my faith. In all of my migrant life I took for granted the practice of putting labels on different groups of people. Much later I saw that labels tend to give us a sense of domination over others since, by categorizing them, we are able to dismiss them, listening or not listening to them, as we choose. In light of this understanding, as I studied and meditated, I determined not to be limited by *or* when *and* was possible. This resolve is why I see myself as both Mexican and American, both English speaking and Spanish speaking, both pietist and activist, both conservative and liberal.

The liberal-conservative controversy was bothersome to me during my days of wandering, when I was wholly unacquainted with a mediating or transcending approach to the subject. It was an immense relief to see that the whole person must include elements of both liberalism and conservatism. Everyone who is intellectually and spiritually alive, open to new truth wherever it may arise, is a liberal. Similarly, everyone who is unwilling, regardless of whatever new trends are sweeping the country, to abandon whatever has proved to be worthwhile, is a conservative. Why I ever felt that I had to choose between these two positions is now inconceivable to me. Liberal and conservative make up a totality that we dare not separate.

When I began to understand that the Christian life need not be divided, a whole new world opened before me. It meant, among other things, that I must be concerned about the spiritual condition of the individual and also about the alteration of a society that allows dehumanization, ignorance, and poverty to exist. I am ready to share prayer with any person and also to discuss ways in which we can overcome the social injustices of his world. William Penn once intimated that we must be changed persons ourselves before we set out to change others. I have found this true in my own life and have witnessed its truth in the lives of others. The changed life begins when we discover our need for spiritual wholeness. Only through a disciplined, continuing nurture of the inner life of the Spirit can a person find an adequate basis of his social concern; and only through his outer life of service can his times of prayer and devotion become honest.

Because of my marriage to James Newby, who belongs to an unbroken Quaker line going back to North Carolina and, before that, to England, my further education has been largely under Quaker auspices. I have studied in Wilmington College, Wilmington, Ohio, and am now a part of the Yokefellow Academy, securing training in creative writing under Dr. D. Elton Trueblood. By living in Cincinnati where my husband is a pastor, I am surrounded by cultural privileges of the highest character, including libraries, museums, art galleries, and symphony concerts. Regular visits to nearby Earlham College at Richmond, Indiana, keep me in touch with a stimulating atmosphere and brilliant minds. Growing up in the back of a truck, I never dreamed of being able to take advantage of the opportunities that are now mine. Now I am entertained in fine houses, read great books, and know of Dr. Samuel Johnson, Blaise Pascal, and other world thinkers through the printed word.

By God's grace I have been drawn into a pattern of living that is quite different from the one I knew as a girl. I enjoy a way of life which my dear mother has never known and of which she has never even dreamed. If I want to see any people whom I admire, I can see them; for in my life there are no barriers of race or class. Such a drastic change in my own life fills me with amazement. Our truck home included no books, and now I am surrounded by books. If I wish to read Plato's *Dialogues* I can do so. I have experienced the liberation of the word.

During my life as a migrant we, of course, traveled through many states all over our beautiful country. However, we never enjoyed or appreciated the history, culture, or even the local beauty of nature around us. We confined ourselves to our camp, and the thought of venturing beyond it was never encouraged. The greatest incentive to living with this self-imposed rule was ignorance.

Everywhere we traveled, there were great libraries with thousands of books that could have introduced us to our rich heritage in our beautiful country. There were, indeed, many cultural opportunities that could have changed our lives; but we never once took advantage of them. Our dreary and ignorant values were the same whether we were in California or Texas or any other state, for we existed only in our small and limited world. It never dawned upon us that we were a part of a larger world and that there were other ways of life open to us or that we had a choice in the way of life we were destined to follow.

Only now, after a few years of marvelous liberation, do I realize the extent of the opportunities from which I was deprived for so long. This awakening makes my heart ache for those who miss the expansions of their horizons and are not even aware that they are missing them. I am saddened when I think of the young men and women who never enter a public library and therefore have no way of freeing themselves from their limited knowledge.

Being liberated from the confines of poverty and of cultural exclusiveness has given me an opportunity to grow without limits in all ways and to minister to the needs of others without being restricted because of national origin, class, or sex. To be accepted by fellow Christians and to be allowed to develop in ways that were once closed to me produce indescribable feelings of joy. Christ has opened the doors, and I have been guided every step of my life in a direction that seeks to break down the restrictive barriers of inhumanity. I have been led to work toward the development of a new world.

The new world of which I speak is one that many dedicated Christians for centuries have been working to establish. I feel that my life is a witness to the tremendous possibilities that this new world can bring. No longer can we classify persons according to economic divisions that work toward the destruction of their humanity and stifle their growth. No longer can we allow the question of race to enter into the evaluation of any person's worth. Christ freed us from these shackles that have been placed on each of us at birth, whether we be rich or poor; white, brown, or black. This is one of the exciting possibilities of the Christian message.

Liberation is not a new word that has just been invented by radical feminists or militant blacks and Chicanos; it is a word that is as old as the Christian message itself. To be truly liberated is to allow Christ to take hold of one's life and to move it beyond the confines of human classifications, preparing it for ministry in a world that is in desperate need of healing. Paul said it perfectly: "For as many of you as were baptized into Christ have put on Christ. There is neither Jew nor Greek, there is neither slave nor free, there is neither male nor female; for you are all one in Christ Jesus" (Gal. 3:27–28, RSV).

The concept that we are all one is essential to the Christian message, while the fact that we all have certain characteristics that distinguish us from our fellows is superficial. I do not mean to play down the importance of individual human qualities or the importance of each one's cultural background. I am proud of my Mexican culture, but I refuse to be bound by it! It seems that in our day we put far too much of our energy into the expression of cultural uniqueness, instead of seeking for those elements in all cultures that can unite us. Christ brought to our world a sanity that, if followed, would liberate us from the dungeons of the separatist philosophy that has overtaken our age and would move us toward the great goal of one world, one humanity.

Why I was brought into a larger life, when so many who were my fellow migrants are still in bondage, I do not know. All I can do is to thank God and try to bring new life to as many others as I possibly can. I cannot let the chain reaction stop with me. To do so would be denial of the purpose that I feel God has intended for my life.

A radically altered view of what a family can be and my entry into a large world in which there are no limits to the ideas which I can entertain and the resources upon which I can draw have turned my life completely around. Because I once lacked the understanding of what a loving family could mean and was limited in my world view and educational resources, I am now thankful for the life into which I have been drawn. This was no small change for a migrant girl, for the contrast between my life then and now is unbelievably great. That I have been completely turned away from the lesser paths which I could have taken cannot be explained except through the grace of God.

To be liberated from the day-to-day struggles of seeking food and shelter, freed to use all of my energy in the Christian ministry, is a beautiful spiritual experience. The concept of being released for ministry is one that has been used by churches for many years. When congregations support their pastors, supplying them with life's basic necessities, they are releasing them for full-time Christian service, for the pastors are thus freed from the need for earning.

I feel that this idea has been illustrated in my own life. As I was released from the struggles of being a migrant, my life was freed to minister as God might direct. I cannot take credit for lifting myself up by my own bootstraps, self-righteously condemning the rest of my people because they do not do the same. What happened to me was a God-given miracle!

I do not know what the remainder of my life will be, but I do know that there is evidence that it is possible to get out of ruts and to start on entirely new paths. I have learned that it is not unreasonable to try to make a new start. I now see clearly that, with God's help, human beings are free to inaugurate ways better than those which they have inherited. I value a long-established heritage, but I also value the vision of how good life can be if we are truly set free.

Epilogue: The Fellowship of Suffering

Since I am a product of both Mexican culture and American culture, and having grown up in both, I retain both in my being. When I left home to go to college I was, in my own way, rejecting the Mexican culture which I had known because, for me, it had become stifling. I was, in fact, suffocating under the extreme male dominance that I had experienced from my father. At that point in my life I could find little good in the Mexican way of life, and I abhorred the violence on which my neighbors thrived. Though I could not remain silent when I witnessed the gross injustices done to the migrant, I recognized that my people remained silent, afraid to say anything for fear they would be put down in the white community (as if they could be put down any more). I wanted to express myself, to get more education, and to be released from the bondage of the stereotype that has been forced upon the Mexican migrant woman. My people could not understand this; and, feeling threatened by my decision, they disowned me. When I was disowned by my family, I really supposed that I had rejected everything about migrant life.

Since that period of turmoil in my life, I have been able to look upon the Mexican migrant culture and to view it more objectively. Although I still reject the violence of the Mexican migrant life and the male dominance of the home, I do not reject other valuable aspects of the subculture that were so much a part of my life while I was growing up. I still love to cook a Mexican meal, complete with tacos, enchiladas, refried beans, Spanish rice, and fruit juice. My husband enjoys Mexican food, too; and since we have been married he has gained thirty pounds! I still use the Spanish language whenever I get a chance, and I am now in the process of teaching our five-year-old daughter my native language. She can count in Spanish and is now working on the names of different types of food. I am anxious for her to acquire a love of Mexican culture and to experience its positive aspects, something that I did not appreciate sufficiently when I was growing up.

I am also very much involved in the struggle for justice in the fields. The sickness and deprivation of the migrant's way of life has been receiving a good deal of publicity lately; and I am anxious to do whatever I can to help secure for my people adequate housing, fair pay, and justice in the courts. The renewed interest in the migrant worker has given me the opportunity to speak before a number of social, church, and civic organizations on "My Life as a Migrant Farm Worker." By so doing, I have become involved more actively than ever before in the personal recovery of many valuable features of the culture. Besides the personal help to me, these speaking engagements seem to be of real educational value to those who know nothing about my people.

I want my readers to understand that in my sincere desire to seek justice for the migrant farm worker, I am by no means following the party line of the affluent suburbanite woman who thinks that she is doing something chic by applying, to her car, a bumper sticker about lettuce. My concern is of a totally different character because I have been there. In short, it is my destiny to be a nonconformist in both the Latin culture and the suburban white culture, with its fashionable causes.

Many Mexican migrants classify me as a *coconut*, a term that denotes any Mexican who has bought into the American culture, rejecting the Mexican heritage received at birth. The coconut is used as a symbol because it is white on the inside and brown on the outside. This is the equivalent to an *Oreo cookie* among American blacks, an *apple* among American Indians, or a *banana* among American Chinese. This is an easy way to classify persons; indeed, it is too easy. Even though I find myself relating for the most part to white society, I have not forgotten my own people.

My recent studies have taught me the importance of wholeness, and this I greatly value; but I have learned something else that I value even more. That is the identification with suffering people wherever and whoever

they are. Three intellectual giants to whom I have been
introduced have been my major teachers in this regard.
One is John Donne of the seventeenth century; another
is John Woolman of the eighteenth century; and the
third is Dr. Albert Schweitzer, whose life has over-
lapped that of many of our contemporaries.

All three of these persons have taught me that I dare
not rejoice in my own release while others are in chains.
It was one of the great moments of my young life when I
sat in the study of Dr. Elton Trueblood, on the Earlham
campus, and read for the first time the *Devotions* of John
Donne. As I sat in that place of exquisite beauty I was,
in an aesthetic sense, very far removed from my home
on wheels. But in another and deeper sense, I was very
close to it. I vowed that however I might be set free, I
would never try to escape. The words of Donne that
reached me most deeply were:

> No man is an island, entire of itself; every man is a piece of
> the continent, a part of the main. If a clod be washed away
> by the sea, Europe is the less, as well as if a manor of thy
> friend's or of thine own were: any man's death diminishes
> me, because I am involved in mankind, and therefore never
> send to know for whom the bell tolls; it tolls for thee.

Later I was equally thrilled when I encountered a
comparable expression of John Woolman, who con-
templated the plight of millions of his fellowmen living
in misery and suddenly realized that he was "mixed
with them." "I saw," he said, "that henceforth I might
not consider myself as a distinct and separate being."

Finally, in reading Dr. Schweitzer's statement of why

he identified himself with the lives of the natives of Africa, I found precisely the expression that I needed:

> He who has been delivered from pain must not think he is now free again, and at liberty to take life up just as it was before, entirely forgetful of the past. He is now a man "whose eyes are open" with regard to pain and anguish, and he must help to overcome those two enemies (so far as human power can control them) and to bring to others deliverance which he himself enjoyed.

Although I have been freed from the life of a migrant and now live under a completely different set of circumstances, the pain and anguish that I experienced as a part of these "forgotten people" remains with me. I must seek deliverance for others who are still traveling the harvest circuit, experiencing, as I once did, the pain and anguish of discrimination and poverty. It is my prayer that this book will serve as a vehicle to enlighten those who can make a difference in the life of the migrant, either through the improvement of conditions under which the migrant must work or by helping him or her get training for more stable, year-round employment.

In my own pilgrimage, I am of course grateful that I have been set free from the dreary, ignorant life of a migrant farm worker; but I know that my freedom must never be complete. It is required of me that I maintain a continued sense of my involvement with my fellow sufferers. In one sense, I am still a migrant, even though I am not a farm worker today. If any of those who are migrants ever see this book, I want them to know that I am still involved in their plight.

Eighteen years ago I was a lonely child, moving as part of a caravan from state to state. There seemed to be no real basis for hope. Though I valued my school friendships, they were quickly lost because I was always moving to another school. Ours is a strange world in many ways, but one of the strangest features of my brief pilgrimage is that I never became totally disheartened. I somehow was able to keep the vision of a changed life before me; and, by a series of curious circumstances, this life finally emerged. The consequence is that I now live in a radically different world from that of my former companions, a world different both spiritually and intellectually. But I am determined that my own undeserved deliverance must never alienate me from the people among whom my life began.

Each day, when I look in the mirror, I am reminded of the heritage I have inherited by the fact of birth. I cannot escape, nor do I wish to escape, my responsibility to my people. Since I once lived the life of a Mexican migrant, it would be wrong to just walk away from it and join another society. Although my life has been altered in many respects, I still remember the hardships I experienced while I was growing up. I never forget the day-to-day struggles for existence; the pain of watching my mother being beaten up by my drunken father; the horror of seeing the blank, dirty faces of children whose stomachs were bloated because there was no food and no one at home to care for them; the long rows of vegetables and fruit that had to be picked; and the back and neck pains that resulted from stooping all day to pick them. One does not just get up and leave the experiences of discrimination that followed us wherever we went, nor the feeling of isolation that surfaced as we were quickly told "our place" in the communities in which we worked. Once having been a part of the Mexican migrant culture, I can never leave it entirely. In short, having been so deeply involved in the fellowship of those who bear the mark of pain, I shall be a part of this fellowship as long as I live.

58889